THE GREAT LIVES SERIES

Great Lives biographies shed an exciting new light on the many dynamic men and women whose actions, visions, and dedication to an ideal have influenced the course of history. Their ambitions, dreams, successes and failures, the controversies they faced and the obstacles they overcame are the true stories behind these distinguished world leaders, explorers, and great Americans.

Other biographies in the Great Lives Series

ACKNOWLEDGMENT

A special thanks to educators Dr. Frank Moretti, Ph.D., Associate Headmaster of the Dalton School in New York City; Dr. Paul Mattingly, Ph.D., Professor of History at New York University; and Barbara Smith, M.S., Assistant Superintendent of the Los Angeles Unified School District, for their contributions to the Great Lives Series.

LECH WALESA
THE ROAD TO DEMOCRACY

Rebecca Stefoff

FAWCETT COLUMBINE
NEW YORK

For middle-school readers

A Fawcett Columbine Book
Published by Ballantine Books

Copyright © 1992 by The Jeffrey Weiss Group, Inc.

Library of Congress Catalog Card Number: 91-72996

ISBN: 978-0-449-90625-5

Cover design and illustration by Paul Davis Studio

Manufactured in the United States of America

145052501

CONTENTS

Lech Walesa as the leader of Solidarity, communist Poland's first independent trade union, 1981. LINDA JAKOB-SON/PHOTOREPORTERS

1

A Strike at the Lenin Shipyard

AS DARKNESS BEGAN to fall on July 31, 1980, bringing the long summer evening to an end, a 36-year-old man named Lech Walesa returned to his home in the city of Gdansk, Poland. It was an apartment on Wrzosy Street in a neighborhood called Stogi, a working-class district hemmed in by factories on one side and a shipping canal on the other. Crowded tenement buildings lined the streets. Next to them were small plots of sandy soil where people grew vegetables. Some had even built ramshackle sheds to house a few chickens or a pig. All in all, Stogi spoke of hard work and hard times. It was a neighborhood, Walesa reflected later, full of people "just waiting for things to improve."

Returning home that evening, however, Lech Walesa may have been wondering whether things would ever get better. Although he was a skilled electrician, he was out of work. He had been fired from three jobs in four years because of his political activities. Walesa was an "oppositionist"—someone who spoke and acted against Poland's ruling Communist party. Over the years, he had witnessed the failure of countless government programs that were supposed to improve people's standard of living. Prices went up while basic items like milk, matches, and sugar grew scarce on store shelves. Sometimes, the police and the army killed workers who protested against unfair working conditions and low wages. Now, Lech Walesa was one of many Poles in Gdansk and elsewhere who spent their afternoons passing out oppositionist leaflets and newspapers that criticized government policies. He had been arrested more than once for this and had grown used to being held in jail for up to 48 hours at a time.

Walesa arrived at the apartment, where he lived with his wife and their five children. It consisted of two small rooms and a tiny kitchen. Several of the children slept in the smaller room, which was only five feet wide. The larger room contained a sofa, a cot, a table, and a sewing machine. Like most working-class Poles, Walesa had waited for years for a better apartment, but Poland was in the grip of a severe housing shortage and the Walesas could afford nothing better on their tight budget.

The little apartment was about to become even more crowded. Walesa's wife, Danuta, was pregnant with their sixth child and close to giving birth. That night, not long after Walesa's return, Danuta went into labor. At almost the same moment, there came a loud knocking on the door.

2

"Open the door, Walesa!" a voice cried. "You are under arrest."

Panic and confusion followed this announcement. Danuta and the children started to cry. Walesa opened the door. Outside stood a commander of the local militia, or military police, with several deputies. They had orders to arrest Walesa for distributing leaflets about the Free Trades Unions (WZZ in Polish), a workers' movement that the government had branded illegal. The arrest in itself was not too frightening. It had happened before. But this one could not have happened at a worse time.

Walesa tried to explain to the militia commander that Danuta was in no condition to be left alone with five children. She had to be taken to the hospital, and then someone would be needed to watch the children. The commander simply ordered his men, "Take him away!"

Terrified and in pain, Danuta screamed at them again and again, begging them not to take her husband away. Her cries echoed down the halls of the apartment building. Torn between obedience to their commander and sympathy for the Walesas' plight, the deputies hesitated.

"Take him away!" the commander barked again. He repeated the order several times. Still the deputies seemed unable to move, and still Danuta cried out in pain and fear. Finally, Walesa tried to bring the situation under control. He agreed to go with the militia quietly if they gave him a chance to calm Danuta. The

3

commander agreed, and Walesa tried to soothe his wife. The Walesas decided that Danuta would ask a neighbor to stay with her until Lech returned from the militia station. Then he left, hoping to be home soon.

The militia held Walesa for 48 hours. By the time he got home, Danuta had been taken to the hospital. She had given birth to their daughter Anna seven hours before Walesa got out of jail.

When he learned this, Walesa was filled with regret. He had been unable to help his wife, and he had missed the birth of his child. "It was a decisive moment for me," he wrote later, "and I swore that from now on I wouldn't let anything intimidate me." Just two weeks later, he had a chance to act upon his newfound resolve.

On the morning of August 14, Walesa rode a streetcar from Stogi to another part of the Gdansk waterfront. During the 35-minute ride, he had plenty of time to think about what he was doing. It was very likely that before the end of the day he would be under arrest once again. He saw an automobile slowly following the streetcar and recognized it as an unmarked car belonging to the Security Bureau (SB), the government's secret police. He was being followed. Surely the SB was well aware that he was on his way to the Lenin Shipyard, where the WZZ had called a workers' strike earlier that morning.

Just about the only way that Polish workers could get the attention of the government was to go on strike—lay down their tools and walk away from their jobs until their demands were met. Such strikes some-

4

times got results—food prices would be lowered, workers' wages would be raised. But these victories were only temporary, for prices always rose again and working conditions seemed to get worse and worse. Furthermore, some of the strikes ended in violent confrontations between the workers and the army or militia. Walesa had seen fellow workers shot down in front of him. Yet he was preparing to join a new strike, because he wanted to be counted among the shipyard workers who were speaking out against the Communist government.

The Lenin Shipyard, one of Poland's biggest shipbuilding operations, was familiar territory to Walesa. He had worked there until 1976, when he had been fired for criticizing the government. He knew many of the workers who were milling around inside the walls of the yard, and he shared their grievances. One concerned food prices, a perpetual problem for Poland's working people. On July 1, the government—which controlled the distribution of food and set all prices—had announced a sharp increase in the price of meat.

Meat was already so costly that many families could afford to eat it only a couple of times a week. Now they would be lucky to eat meat once a week, and some people would be unable to afford it at all. The population was outraged by this price increase. People became even angrier when they heard rumors that Poland was sending meat to the Soviet Union, where the 1980 Summer Olympic Games were being held in Moscow. They were furious that food produced in their country could be sent away to feed athletes from all around the world, instead of being used to feed people at home.

This and other economic and political problems created a feeling of unrest among the general population. But the shipyard workers also had another, more specific reason to strike. Just a few days earlier, the managers of the yard had fired an employee named Anna Walentynowicz. She was a 51-year-old widow who had worked at the yard for 30 years, first as a welder and then as the operator of a crane. Walentynowicz knew everyone at the yard, and people liked her. She was especially popular with the younger workers, the boys and young men who were far from their homes and families. She gave them motherly advice and they called her Pani Ania ("Mrs. Ania"). The other shipyard employees knew that Walentynowicz was a good, careful worker. She had been fired because she was an oppositionist, a member of the WZZ.

The WZZ prepared leaflets that gave the facts about Walentynowicz's dismissal. "We are calling on you to defend Anna Walentynowicz!" they read. "If we fail many of you will soon find yourselves in the same position."

Early on August 14, three 20-year-old supporters of the WZZ passed these leaflets out on streetcars and at train stations along routes leading to the shipyard. By the time the workers arrived at the yard, most of them had received one, or seen the posters that the three young men carried.

At the sprawling Lenin Shipyard, WZZ supporters held aloft banners and posters and began a march

6

through the various sections of the huge operation. As they marched, they called out to their fellow workers to join them. Spurred by the WZZ members among them, some workers decided to rally around Walentynowicz. They laid down their blowtorches and hammers and joined the march. Soon the strikers had assembled near the main gate of the yard. They called out their demands: a pay raise, a promise that they would not be punished for striking, and a monument to honor workers who had been shot by the militia in an earlier strike. They also demanded that the yard managers give jobs back to Walentynowicz and other employees who had been dismissed for political reasons.

Walesa reached the shipyard at this point and quickly understood the situation. Outside the yard, security guards were checking the passes of everyone who went through the gates. Inside the yard, the strikers were milling about, listening to a man who was standing on a bulldozer. Walesa recognized the speaker as Klemens Gniech, the current director of the shipyard. Gniech was a persuasive speaker who was popular with the workers. Walesa feared that Gniech might talk the strikers into ending their protest before it really got under way. Walesa felt a sense of urgency; it was time for him to get in there and speak up.

But he had no pass to get into the shipyard. It had been taken away from him years before when he was fired. So he ran to the rear of the yard and climbed over the 12-foot wall. At that moment, Gniech was promising the strikers that he would discuss all their demands—*after* they returned to work. He urged them to end the strike peacefully and go back to their jobs. The strikers were uncertain. They knew, of course, that promises from the yard management were not always kept, but at the same time many of them were afraid they might lose their jobs—or worse, be attacked by the militia—if they stayed on strike. The crowd muttered, wavered, and then began to break up. It seemed that the momentum of the strike was lost.

Just then a short, stocky man with a bushy brown mustache jumped up onto the bulldozer right behind Gniech. It was Walesa. He tapped Gniech on the shoulder and said, "Remember me? I worked here for ten years, and I still feel I'm a shipyard worker." Many of the workers knew Walesa and cheered when he turned to speak to them. With passion ringing in his voice, he called for the strike to continue. The cheering grew even louder. Then Walesa cried out that the workers would not move from where they stood until their demands were met. The workers, their excitement on the rise again, backed him up with loud cries of agreement.

Walesa's speech from the bulldozer reached out to the hearts and minds of his listeners. "When Lech made his speeches," his friend and associate Mieczyslaw Wachowski later recalled, "it was as if he was riding the crest of a wave rolling in from the crowd, riding it like a surfer. He was able to express what each of us felt deep inside. This was what cemented the crowd together in his favor. At last here was someone who expressed the thoughts of the man in the street!"

On that morning of August 14, 1980, Walesa's words

fired the enthusiasm of the Lenin Shipyard workers, giving them renewed strength and a sense of commitment. The strike was on.

But Walesa's call to action accomplished more than he or anyone else ever dreamed possible. It was heard not just in the city of Gdansk, but throughout Poland and around the world. Ultimately, it brought about tremendous changes in Polish society. It launched Lech Walesa into a new and historic role as the leader of a movement called Solidarity. It helped pave the way for democracy in Poland. And eventually, it made Lech Walesa the president of his country.

2

Poland's History of Struggle

O UNDERSTAND WHY Lech Walesa became an oppositionist, it is necessary to know something about Poland's heritage and its long struggle for freedom. The events of Walesa's life occurred within the framework of Polish history, which in turn has been shaped by geography.

Poland is in eastern Europe. It is bordered on the north by the Baltic Sea, an arm of the Atlantic Ocean. This stretch of seacoast is important to Poland because it has good ports for shipping. One of them is Gdansk, Walesa's home and the birthplace of the Solidarity movement. On the south, Poland is bordered by Czechoslovakia. But the neighbors that have played the most important roles in Poland's history are Germany, to the west, and Russia (now the Soviet Union), to the east.

Among the major features of the Polish landscape are the Vistula River, which flows through the country from south to north and empties into the Baltic Sea, and the mountain ranges in the southern part of the

10

country, where coal and other minerals are mined. Poland has an area of 120,727 square miles, making it slightly smaller than the state of New Mexico in the United States. At various times in the past, however, Poland's area has been larger and its borders have been quite different than they are today. Until 1945, part of what is now western Poland belonged to Germany, and eastern Poland included territory that now belongs to the Soviet Union.

About 2,000 years ago, people from various Slavic language groups, members of a dozen or more closely related ethnic groups that originated in eastern Europe and western Russia, began forming communities in what is now Poland. The name Poland (*Polska* in Polish) comes from the Slavic word *polanie,* or "plains people," and referred to the groups that settled in the lowlands and plains of northern Europe.

Poland's population was not large at first—probably about a million people by the tenth century A.D. Around that time, the groups living along the Vistula River were united under a dynasty, or royal family, called the Piasts, and the history of the Polish nation began. King Mieszko I of the Piast dynasty was confronted with aggressive German princes on his western frontier. To hold them at bay, he agreed to become a Christian. This would make Poland part of the Holy Roman Empire and bring Polish lands under the protection of the Pope, the head of the Roman Catholic church.

King Mieszko was baptized, and his subjects followed suit. From that time on, the Poles were a fervently Catholic people who regarded their country as the eastern frontier of the Holy Church. To their east, in Russia and Turkey (then part of the Ottoman empire), were two alien religions. The Russians belonged to the Eastern Orthodox church, which was Christian but had split away from the Roman Catholic church, and the Turks were followers of Islam, a non-Christian faith born in Arabia. A few centuries later, when Germany came under the sway of the new Protestant religions, the Catholic Poles were squeezed between two powerful neighbors who did not share their religious beliefs. This fostered a feeling of isolation among the Polish people, combined with pride in their strong faith.

In the meantime, Poland underwent political changes. For several centuries, the young nation was torn by conflicts. Within the country, members of the royal family quarreled over land and power. Poland also fought border wars. In the west it battled German princes. In the east, hordes of Mongol warriors had invaded Russia from the steppes of Asia. Finally, in the fourteenth century, Casimir III, the last king of the Piast dynasty, ended the conflicts within the royal family and united the country once again. Casimir the Great, as he was called by his people, made peace with the German princes on the western border and also welcomed Jewish refugees into Poland. Under his rule, Poland's laws were organized into a legal code and a university was founded in the city of Krakow. Casimir the Great held the throne from 1333 until 1370—a golden age for medieval Poland.

After Casimir's death, Poland merged its ruling family with that of a state called the Grand Duchy of Lithuania. The union extended Polish territory north along the coast of the Baltic Sea, west into German territory, and as far east into Russia as the Black Sea. This marked the greatest extent of Polish sovereignty. But in the sixteenth century, the union was threatened by quarrels between the Polish and Lithuanian nobles. To preserve unity, the nobility created a parliament, which they called the Sejm, thus beginning an era that has been called Poland's Noble Democracy.

All the nobles of the kingdom were members of the Sejm, and they elected the king by vote, holding their elections in a large field outside the city of Warsaw. So at a time when most of Europe was governed by kings and emperors who claimed to rule by divine right, Poland had a form of democratic government. It was not a true democracy in the modern sense of the word, because only the land-owning aristocracy voted in the Sejm. Peasants in the countryside, as well as laborers and merchants in the towns and cities, had no say at all in how the kingdom was ruled or by whom. Yet Poland's Noble Democracy was extraordinary for its time. It reflected the radical ideas that a king had to have the approval of the people he governed and that leadership should be decided by vote.

The nobles—called *szlachta* in Polish—who made up the Sejm were passionately devoted to the ideas of liberty and equality (although they applied these principles only to their own class and not to society as a whole). They had such high regard for their own individual rights and liberties that they allowed a single

13

negative vote to veto motions in the Sejm. This meant that any member of the Sejm could say "No" to a proposed law or measure, and that law or measure would be blocked. This system gave much weight to individual opinions, but it also made it difficult to get things done, because agreement among all the *szlachta* was rare.

The century or so that followed the establishment of the Sejm was another golden era in Poland's history. Literature, science, the arts, and scholarship flourished in the kingdom. Poland was known throughout Europe as a liberal, advanced, humane country. Yet the same democratic system that made Poland an enlightened kingdom eventually caused its downfall. Because the Sejm elected the king, the nobles became more powerful than he. Soon the *szlachta* were strong enough to deny the king permission to have an army. They did this to keep him from becoming powerful enough to take control of the country on his own. But all of Poland's neighbors were ruled by powerful leaders with large armies, and they grew stronger as Poland grew weaker. During the seventeenth and eighteenth centuries, Poland was defeated in wars with Sweden, Russia, and Austria (at that time, Austria was the center of the Austro-Hungarian empire, which included present-day Czechoslovakia). The Polish government was also weakened by a bloody peasant uprising in the region called the Ukraine, which is now part of the Soviet Union but formerly belonged to Poland.

These attacks from within and without eroded Po-

14

land's strength. As the end of the eighteenth century approached, the kingdom could no longer defend itself against the aggressive nations around it. Polish territory began to be divided among Russia, Germany (at the time known as Prussia), and Austria. These divisions were called partitions, and there were three of them: in 1772, in 1793, and in 1795. After the partition of 1795, Poland had vanished. It no longer appeared on the map of Europe. Everything that had once been Poland had been gobbled up by its three neighbors. The city of Warsaw was now part of Russia. Krakow, in the south, was part of the Austro-Hungarian empire. Gdansk in the north and Poznan in the west belonged to Germany. The three powers went so far as to sign a treaty in which they agreed that the country of Poland would never again be allowed to exist.

The partitions had a profound effect on the people who lived in what had once been Poland. They did not stop thinking of themselves as Poles just because their state had been taken over and erased from the map. Poland remained the country of their hearts. Parents told their children tales of Polish glories in "the old days." Polish poets and playwrights, many of them living in exile in other lands, wrote works that glorified Polish history and culture. Keeping the Polish language alive was an act of rebellion, and loyalty to the Roman Catholic church became a form of patriotism. For generations, every Pole dreamed of the day when Poland would be born again.

The Poles did more than just dream. They fought to liberate their homeland. In 1794, 1830, 1848, 1863,

15

and again in 1905 they rose up in arms against the Russians, who were the worst oppressors. Each uprising was crushed with brutal force by the troops of the Russian czar, or emperor. But the Polish rebels who fought in the uprisings became heroes, and many Polish families passed down stories of a grandfather's, father's, or uncle's exploits in one of the rebellions. Two of Lech Walesa's great-great-uncles, for example, fought against the Russians in the uprising of 1863 and spent many years in exile in Siberia, in northeastern Russia, as punishment. Walesa recalls hearing stories about these ancestors while he was growing up.

In the early twentieth century, all of Europe underwent political convulsions, and Poland was no exception. World War I (1914–1918) brought sweeping changes to the nations of Europe. Germany and Austria-Hungary went to war against Russia. In Russia, the Bolshevik Revolution overthrew the czar and introduced communism to what became known as the Soviet Union. With all these countries fighting among themselves, the leader of Poland's independence movement, a military officer named Jozef Pilsudski, declared Poland independent.

The war ended when the forces of France, Great Britain, and the United States prevailed over those of Germany and Austria-Hungary. The Treaty of Versailles, which formally ended World War I, made Poland a sovereign state once again. The end of the war ushered in a time of great pride, thanksgiving, and hope for Poles. For the first time in 123 years, the Polish nation appeared on the map of Europe. Pilsudski assumed power as marshal, the chief of state of the new republic.

Independence had been won, but the reborn nation faced an immediate threat. For centuries, the agricultural provinces just east of the present-day border between Poland and the Soviet Union had been desired by both nations. Now the new Polish state and the Soviet Union both claimed possession of them. Pilsudski declared that Poland was ready to fight to regain its former territories, saying grandly, "Poland will be a great power, or she will not exist." The two countries went to war over these territories in 1919. The Polish army marched into the Soviet Union, advancing as far as Kiev, and the Soviet army counterattacked on Poland's eastern frontier.

By the summer of 1920, the Soviets had the upper hand. They had pushed the Polish army back to the Vistula River and almost to Warsaw. But that August the tide turned in favor of Poland, in a battle that Poles call "the Miracle on the Vistula." United in their opposition to the advancing Soviets, the common people of Poland took up arms and fought side by side with the army. The Polish forces, which had been on the brink of defeat, succeeded in driving the Soviets back across the border. The Treaty of Riga, signed in 1921, ended the war and established Poland's eastern border with the Soviet Union.

The years after the war saw the blossoming of a cultural renaissance in the newly independent Poland. Painters, writers, musicians, and historians were filled

17

with excitement now that they were no longer repressed by foreign powers. The cities and universities experienced an outpouring of creative and scholarly activity. Many Poles today view the 1920s as another of Poland's golden ages. Yet despite all the jubilation that national independence brought, Poland had many problems.

For one thing, Pilsudski claimed that the country was a free republic, but he ruled with almost absolute power, in the manner of a dictator. For another, the country's economy was in very poor shape. Much of the countryside had been devastated by the battles of World War I and the Polish-Soviet War. To make matters worse, the retreating German and Soviet armies had carried out a program of destruction and looting. They had stripped many factories and workshops of their machinery and equipment, and money was too scarce in the postwar years to rebuild Polish industry. Unemployment was high, and the standard of living, especially for rural peasants, lagged far behind that of other Europeans. Country villages lacked clean water and electricity. Some workers' neighborhoods in the cities were becoming dirty, overcrowded slums.

Although Poles were overjoyed to have achieved national independence, they did not agree on how the country should be run. Many supported Pilsudski, the hero of the Miracle on the Vistula. Others, however, began to say that perhaps Poland needed new leadership. Political parties formed. Some of the new parties were concerned with the issue of land reform, one of the most pressing political and economic concerns of postwar Poland. More than 75 percent of all Poles lived in the countryside, but very few of them owned their land. Nearly all of the land was owned by about 1 percent of the population. The landowners lived comfortably on large estates or in the cities and employed peasants to work their fields. Such laborers often had only small gardens for their own use. Disgusted with this state of affairs, activists among the peasantry formed the Peasant party and called for fairer distribution of the land.

Another new party was the Polish Socialist party (PPS in Polish), which wanted to see Poland adopt the economic system known as socialism. The ideals of socialism were lofty: to abolish poverty, to ensure employment for all, and to create a society in which everyone received equal benefits from the state. The principles by which these goals were to be achieved included the redistribution of wealth, the end of class distinctions in society, and control of land and factories by the workers. The communist regime in the Soviet Union was based on socialism. The Soviet Union had started out as a Marxist-Leninist state; its political and economic systems were based on the principles of socialism set forth by Karl Marx and the principles of communist government enacted by Soviet leader V. I. Lenin. A later, sterner version of communism, called Stalinism after Soviet premier Joseph Stalin, introduced the widespread use of force, terror, and execution to control the population and crush dissent.

Some Poles felt that socialism might be the answer

to the country's problems. All Poles, however, rejected the Soviet brand of communism. They did not want to be dominated by the Soviet Union's Communist party. The Polish people, in fact, were determined to reject everything Soviet—after all, for generations they had regarded Russians as their worst enemies. That feeling would not disappear overnight, and the recent border war had made the Polish people more hostile than ever to Soviet influences and ideas.

Pilsudski died in 1935, and for a few years the government tried to cope with Poland's troubled economy and growing political unrest. Then, just 20 years after achieving independence, Poland was once more faced with a threat from beyond its borders. The Soviet Union and Nazi Germany, on the verge of going to war with one another, made a secret agreement to divide Poland between them. When World War II broke out, Poland was overrun by the armies of its neighbors and once again disappeared from the maps of Europe.

3

In the Shadow of War

GERMANY TRIGGERED WORLD War II by invading Poland on September 1, 1939. The attack was a *blitzkreig*, or lightning-fast war; in little more than a week, the German military machine had destroyed Poland's defenses and taken over the country. Poles in Warsaw resisted, hoping against hope for British, French, or American aid, until the Soviet army marched across Poland's eastern border on September 17. The two powers proceeded to divide Poland into zones of occupation before going to war with each other in 1941.

The people of occupied Poland suffered terribly under both the Nazis and the Soviets. In German-occupied Poland, some 3 million Jews—about 90 percent of Poland's Jewish population—were herded into concentration camps such as Auschwitz, where nearly all of them were killed. An additional 3 million non-Jewish Poles were killed as well. These included priests, teachers, writers, and community leaders who were thought to pose a danger to Nazi domination.

Matters were also dreadful in the Soviet-dominated parts of Poland. The Soviet secret police rounded up Polish soldiers and army officers, priests, teachers, and prominent citizens and sent them to labor camps in distant, primitive Siberia. At least 1 million Poles—about 10 percent of the population of Soviet-occupied Poland—were deported to Siberia, and fewer than half of them ever returned.

In the middle of the war, on September 29, 1943, Lech Walesa was born in the tiny village of Popowo in the Dobrzyn region of Poland. The Walesa family had been living in Dobrzyn since Mateusz Walesa, Lech's great-great-grandfather, settled there sometime in the late eighteenth or early nineteenth century, in the early years of Poland's first partition.

The name Walesa means "he who roams," and according to family legends, Mateusz had been a roamer. The Walesas believe that he had spent some time in France, or Italy, or perhaps even the United States before settling in Dobrzyn. At any rate, he had acquired a substantial fortune, which he used to buy an estate of about 400 acres. The estate included almost all of the village of Popowo. As the chief landowner and owner of the local inn, food shop, and pub, Mateusz Walesa was a person of considerable importance in the community.

Mateusz raised a large family, and at his death, according to Polish custom, his property was divided in equal shares among his children. In 1863, two of Mateusz's sons, Konstanty and Wincenty, fought in the Polish uprising against Russia and were exiled to

Siberia. Tales about the heroic exploits of these ancestors were woven into Lech's childhood. Lech's great-grandfather was Mateusz's eldest son, Jan. Fearful that the Russians would punish him for his brothers' part in the rebellion, Jan fled to France, where distant relatives of Mateusz were living. Jan Walesa liked France so much that he stayed there, gambling in the casinos and generally enjoying himself. He came back to Poland once in a while to sell some land in order to pay his gambling debts, but he left the management of his steadily diminishing Polish estate in the hands of his wife and children.

The eldest of these children, also named Jan, was Lech Walesa's grandfather. Upon the senior Jan's death, the younger Jan received an inheritance of 50 acres. Like his father, however, he had a taste for gambling and for life abroad. Lech Walesa reports that his grandfather spent more time in France, frittering away what was left of the family fortune in the gambling casinos, than at home in Poland. Eventually Jan ran out of money. First he had to dismiss the family's single servant because he could no longer afford to pay her wages, then he sold almost all of his remaining land. Finally, he settled down at home and raised his very large family. By now the Walesas were an extremely poor family, no longer the local gentry.

Jan Walesa, though, took a great interest in the world outside Popowo. Lech Walesa's older sister Izabela remembers their grandfather as a strong-minded, bushy-mustached, jovial old fellow who liked to reminisce about his youthful adventures in Paris.

Too poor to buy cigarettes, he took to rolling his own tobacco in a scrap of torn newspaper—but he always read every line of the paper first. Among the local people, Jan Walesa had the reputation of being "a political man." He was said to have been a member of Marshal Pilsudski's underground resistance movement during World War I, and to the end of his days he treasured a yellowing photograph of himself with Pilsudski.

Less certain is the actual role Jan Walesa played in Polish affairs. He used to tell how he had once saved Pilsudski's life by disguising him in a woman's dress and hiding him from the Russians. Although such an incident did occur in Pilsudski's career, historians say that Jan Walesa had nothing to do with it. An elderly neighbor in Popowo who remembered Jan well once said to Lech Walesa, "That episode with Pilsudski was pure fancy; he was just trying to brag."

Jan Walesa's two eldest sons did fight with Pilsudksi at the Vistula River in August of 1920. One was captured by the Soviets and sent to Siberia. The family received two letters from him, describing the miseries of life in Siberia and the cruelty of the Soviet authorities. After that he was never heard from again. The other son died in a battle not far from Popowo. Village legend says that he could have escaped, but was killed when he went back to his fallen horse to get some gold that he had hidden under the saddle. Lech's father, Boleslaw, was 12 years old at the time and took no part in the fighting.

At Jan Walesa's death, his remaining property was divided among his surviving children. Boleslaw received a few acres of poor soil, not very good for farming. Boleslaw Walesa was a tall, powerfully built man, with penetrating eyes under thick, dark brows. He fell in love with a girl named Feliksa Kaminska. Feliksa's parents were well-to-do, cultivated people. Her mother was a well-read woman who had lived in the United States and owned the area's largest collection of books. Her father was the keeper of the parish records. The Kaminskis were not eager to see their youngest daughter married to the son of a family that had gambled away its fortune, but Miss Fela, as Boleslaw called the girl, had faith in Boleslaw's ability to provide a good life for her. In spite of her parents' opposition, the two were married.

Boleslaw was able to grow some wheat and potatoes on his little plot of ground, but he realized he could not hope to support a family that way. Soon after his marriage, he went into the construction business with his brothers Zygmunt and Izydor. They were quite successful, building churches, houses, cattle sheds, and barns in Popowo and other villages nearby. In 1934, a daughter was born to Boleslaw and Feliksa, and they named her Izabela. For three years little Iza lived with her Kaminski grandparents on their farm while her parents lived in a shed on Boleslaw's land. Then, in 1937, Feliksa bore a second child, a boy who was named Edward, and the Walesa family moved into a tiny family house. In 1939, they had a third child. They named the boy Stanislaw, after one of Boleslaw's brothers. That was the year that World War II broke out.

25

The Walesa family, like all Polish families, was touched by the war. At the end of August 1939, just before Germany invaded Poland, Boleslaw Walesa and his brother Stanislaw were called into the Polish army. After the invasion, they were taken prisoner by the Germans, but they were allowed to return home after a few months. By then, the Dobrzyn region was occupied by the Germans. The Nazis closed or destroyed village schools and libraries and took control of the big farms. Small properties like the Walesas' were left alone, but many of the men were forced into work crews to build German military fortifications. Among them, Boleslaw's brother Stanislaw was rounded up and taken to a German labor camp.

In 1943, Stanislaw escaped. He fled into the woods near Popowo, where many Polish men were hiding. They had formed an underground resistance group and vowed to fight against the Nazis. Although the Germans severely punished anyone caught aiding these resistance fighters, many of the villagers helped when they could. Feliksa often gave the nine-year-old Izabela food or blankets to leave in a certain place near the forest, since children could get past the German guards more easily than adults.

One day not long after Stanislaw's escape from the camp, Nazi officers came to Boleslaw and Feliksa's house. Izabela was so frightened that she ran into the woods and hid there with her brother Edward. By the time the children returned to the house, their father was gone. The Nazis had taken him in for questioning, in spite of the fact that Feliksa was pregnant and could not tend the farm alone. Boleslaw was still a Nazi prisoner in late September, when his fourth child was born. Feliksa named the boy Lech.

Later that winter, the Nazis rounded up all the men of the region, including those who had been hiding in the forest. Stanislaw and other prisoners who had run away from the Nazi work camps were sent to a concentration camp. Boleslaw was equally unfortunate. He was beaten and then forced to dig ditches and build bridges for the Germans. During the winter of 1944–45, the working conditions were appalling. The men were housed in unheated barracks, and Boleslaw, already weak from the beating, developed a hacking cough. It was clear that he was suffering from a serious lung disease, but he received no medical treatment. Finally, when the Germans finished work at that site and moved the men on to another camp, Boleslaw was left behind, almost too weak to move, with only a thin sheet to warm him. He caught pneumonia, but he recovered enough to make his way home.

Boleslaw returned to Popowo in the spring of 1945. For the first time, he saw his son Lech, who was a year and a half old. But Boleslaw knew that his life was almost over. He coughed constantly and hemorrhaged blood from his lungs. He managed to hang on until May, when his brother Stanislaw returned from the labor camp. On his deathbed, Boleslaw made Stanislaw promise to take care of Feliksa and the children. Then he died.

While the Walesas were suffering this family tragedy, the Soviet Red Army steadily pushed the Germans

27

west across Poland. Many Poles, desperate to help liberate their country from the Nazis, fought alongside the Soviets and a Polish army was formed under Soviet command.

Poland had two governments at this time. One was a government-in-exile, which consisted of Polish leaders who had fled to London to escape the invading armies in 1939. The other was the Polish Committee of National Liberation, which was created in the Polish city of Lublin by Stalin and the Communist party of the Soviet Union. The Lublin Committee, as this government was called, consisted of Polish communists. The United States and other Western nations felt that the government-in-exile was the real ruling body of Poland, while the Soviet Union, of course, backed the Lublin Committee. In Poland, a group of Poles loyal to the government-in-exile formed a resistance force called the Home Army. However, the Lublin Committee was supported by the powerful Red Army of the Soviet Union, as well as the Polish army that was under Soviet command.

As the Germans were driven west, it became clear that the Soviets were not going to liberate Poland. Instead they were going to make it their own. The Soviet-commanded forces would not aid the Home Army, even though both groups were battling the Nazis. When members of the Home Army emerged from their hiding places as the Germans retreated, they were promptly arrested and executed by the Soviet secret police.

The crisis came in August 1944. The Soviet army was approaching the city of Warsaw, which was still occupied by the Germans. The government-in-exile in London decided that the Home Army should try to liberate Warsaw before the Soviets could do so. This would let the exiled leaders return in triumph to Poland's capital. Perhaps then they could expel the Soviets from the rest of Poland.

On August 1, the Home Army launched a brave but doomed uprising in Warsaw. The resistance fighters were inadequately armed, and they stood no chance against Germany's army, which was powerful even in retreat. The Germans got out of Warsaw unharmed by roping Polish women and children to the sides of their tanks to stop the resistance fighters from firing at them. Then they began to systematically bomb the city into rubble. All the while, the Soviet army waited a few miles away, doing nothing to help the Polish fighters.

Battered almost out of existence, the Home Army surrendered on October 2. The Nazis carried the entire remaining population of Warsaw off to concentration camps and then blew up the schools, churches, homes, and buildings that were still standing after the bombings. When the Soviets advanced into the empty streets of Warsaw, in January 1945, they found that more than 90 percent of the ancient and historic city had been destroyed.

The war ended in 1945, but Poland did not return to its prewar independence. Its fate was determined by deals made among the victorious Allied nations: Great Britain, the United States, France, and the Soviet Union. The Allies agreed that Europe would be divided into several "spheres of influence," with Poland in the

Soviet Union's sphere. The Soviet Union proposed new borders for Poland that would, in effect, move the country about 150 miles to the west. This gave the Soviet Union those fertile grain-growing territories in eastern Poland that it had lost in the Polish-Soviet War. Poland's lost territory was replaced with land taken from Germany in the west.

The Soviet Union also insisted upon installing the Lublin Committee as the official government of Poland. Because the other Allies did not want to make an enemy of the Soviet Union, they agreed to these terms, insisting only that the people of Poland be allowed to hold free elections soon. Many Poles felt—and continue to feel—that they were betrayed by President Franklin D. Roosevelt and Prime Minister Winston Churchill, the wartime leaders of the United States and Great Britain.

The promised elections did not take place until 1947, and when they did take place, they were not free. Many of the candidates were picked by the Soviet Communist party or by Polish leaders who had come under the influence of the Soviets. People were pressured to vote as the communists wanted them to vote. Whole factories full of workers were marched to the polls and told that they would be fired if they did not vote for the government's pet candidates. As a result of this and other tactics, communist candidates won 80 percent of the votes and took full control of the government. In the following year, the Polish Socialist party (PPS) and the communist Polish Workers' party were merged into a single party, the Polish United Workers' party

(PZPR in Polish), which was controlled by the Soviet Communist party.

The Soviet-dominated communist governments that came to power throughout Eastern Europe after World War II were modeled on the government of the Soviet Union itself. The most powerful person in each country was the head, or secretary, of that country's communist party, which acknowledged the leadership of the Soviet Communist party. In the Soviet system, the policies and decisions of party leaders were carried out by two administrative systems, or bureaucracies: the party and the state political organization. Of the two, the party had more real power, because the party chose the candidates who were elected to political office.

In addition to the full-time party officials, there was a large body of people who were loyal to the party. This group was called the *nomenklatura* ("the trusted ones"), an elite group given all the important and influential jobs in the country: army officer, college professor, schoolteacher, banker, newspaper publisher or editor, police or fire captain, leader of a student group or a women's club. People high in the party's favor—the *nomenklatura* and their families—had privileges that were not available to the general population. They not only got the best jobs, but also the available apartments and cars. These people formed an upper class, even though communism was supposed to produce a classless society.

By Stalin's time, the original ideals of communism had been swallowed up by the complex party bureaucracy. The state was all-powerful and exercised complete control over individuals' lives. Religion was banned, and anything that might draw people's loyalty away from the party was outlawed. The party compiled long lists of troublemakers or dissidents. Privacy disappeared. Secret police were everywhere, watching and listening. Everyone was answerable to the party and subject to its orders at all times. It was impossible to change apartments or jobs, get married, travel, or go to college without the party's permission. Everyone had to carry identification papers. Anyone caught without his or her government-issued documents could be arrested. And it was next to impossible to get anything done, whether it was applying for a travel pass to visit relatives or trying to have a telephone installed in an apartment, without negotiating a mind-numbing maze of bureaucratic agencies and their endless paperwork.

Each Eastern European country that came under communist rule was supposed to be Sovietized—that is, the government and party were supposed to match the Soviet model. Industries and utilities were to be turned over to the state, and privately owned farms were to be merged into group farms, or collectives. The state would tell farmers what crops to grow and factories what goods to produce. It would dictate who could buy and sell goods, and it would set workers' wages and the prices for all goods and services. But the crushing hand of Sovietization lay less heavily on Poland than on some other nations.

The PZPR never became as powerful as the Soviet Union's Communist party. Somehow Poland was able to keep a fair share of its own traditions and national character alive. For example, the communists were never able to outlaw religion, and the Roman Catholic church remained a vital part of Polish life. The PZPR executed some outspoken priests and church officials and sent others to prison, but this martyrdom only strengthened the church's hold on people's hearts. Poland was the only nation in postwar Eastern Europe where young people remained as fervently religious as their parents and grandparents had been.

Another aspect of Sovietization that never took hold in Poland was collective farming. Ten years after the war, only 9 percent of Poland's farms had been merged into collectives. The Poles remained stubbornly individualistic. The majority also remained nationalistic and patriotic, every bit as opposed to Russian domination as their ancestors had been. Stalin, the Soviet leader, went so far as to say that bringing communism to Poland was like putting a saddle on a cow—you could tie it on, but it just did not seem to fit.

Poland's first communist leader after the war was Wladyslaw Gomulka. The Soviets took Gomulka out of office in 1948 because they felt he was not trying hard enough to Sovietize the country. Then they put him in jail because his loyalty to Stalin was in doubt. His replacement was Boleslaw Bierut, who did not hesitate to take orders from the Soviet Union. The state made its most earnest attempts to Sovietize Poland during Bierut's time in office.

All the while, in Popowo, far from the center of national affairs, Lech Walesa was growing up. The most significant event in his early family life occurred about a year after his father's death, when his mother married his uncle Stanislaw. This was in keeping with Boleslaw Walesa's dying wish that Stanislaw take care of Feliksa and the children, but Boleslaw's children never really accepted their mother's remarriage. Lech remembers that for a short time the four children ran off into the woods, refusing even to see their stepfather. Izabela especially resented Stanislaw, because she had the clearest memories of their father. Walesa feels that his mother was not particularly happy with Stanislaw, but Stanislaw did fulfill his promise. He built a stone house for the family, worked hard at several jobs, and tried to treat all seven of his children and stepchildren fairly.

Times were difficult in Poland during Lech's childhood, and food was scarce. Stanislaw grew crops and raised some livestock on his four acres, but each year he had to give a portion of what he produced to the government. What was left over was barely enough to feed everyone. Bread was often unavailable in Popowo, even at harvest time, and Lech remembers that his family sometimes went for several months without tasting a crumb of it. A slice of bread with butter or lard was a treat, and meat was served only once a week. Most meals consisted of noodles. The family kept a cow for milk, and the children learned to gather mushrooms and apples in the forest and to net fish in the local ponds.

Every child had chores to do. At age five, a child would be assigned to tend the geese; at age seven, to

34

take the cow to pasture; at age ten, to tend all the livestock and do other jobs. Every afternoon, Lech spent two hours chopping straw into small pieces to feed the animals. Years of walking on coarse straw in his bare feet gave him corns and calluses that are painful to this day. To earn a little money to help pay for clothes and shoes, Lech and his brothers also did extra chores on their neighbors' farms, and during school vacations they worked for a local brickmaker.

Lech did not look forward to the life of a farmer. He hated the uncertainty of living off the land. "You never knew whether something would grow or whether it would get eaten up by insects or pecked up by birds," he recalled later.

Religion and politics were part of family life, and both shaped Lech's character. His mother was devoutly religious. She led prayers at the foot of a statue of the Virgin Mary in the village, and each Sunday she led the children on the two-mile walk to church. Lech had deep religious feelings from earliest childhood. "My faith can almost be said to have flowed into me with my mother's milk," he has written.

Lech's stepfather was not a particularly political man, but he listened to the news of the world on a battery-powered shortwave radio every evening. Lech eagerly listened along. With voices from the radio crackling in his ear, he felt connected to people and events around the world, and he gained a lasting respect for communication and the free exchange of information.

The other major element of Lech's early life was

35

school. Lech started school at age seven. He was not an outstanding student, but he did well at sports. He still remembers with pride that he won third prize—a ball of real leather—in a regional archery contest. Most of the time, the village children played soccer and other games with bundles of old rags.

Lech loved after-school games. "I didn't stand out much from the other pupils," he admits, "and I didn't really spring into life until the last bell rang." He liked showing off and trying to outdo his friends. In the summer they would plunge into a pond or lake and see who could swim out farthest from the shore. In winter they would hop from one ice floe to another across the freezing water, again to see who would go farthest. Lech won many of these contests.

In July 1956, when Lech was a schoolboy of 12, an event occurred that shook the Polish nation. This was a protest by workers at an engineering plant in the city of Poznan. Outraged at low wages and high food prices, an angry mob took to the streets with banners that read "Bread and Freedom" and "Russians Go Home." The military police were called out to quell the demonstration—and they did so, after two days of street fighting in which dozens of people were killed and hundreds were injured.

The Poznan riots showed that the people were dangerously discontented with the government, and that shook up Poland's communist bureaucrats. They decided that Poland needed a leader who had popular support, so they turned Bierut out of office and restored Gomulka as party secretary. The Polish people were inclined to think well of Gomulka because he had been imprisoned by the Soviets, and for a time it appeared that matters would improve under his leadership. But the most lasting effect of the Poznan riots was that the Polish workers had learned that they could capture the attention of the government. If they were willing to put their lives on the line, they could even drive the party secretary out of power. These events were to be repeated in later years, with Lech Walesa as one of the angry workers. The Poznan demonstration is now considered to be the birth of Poland's labor movement, the movement that Walesa would someday lead.

Walesa's school days came to an end in 1958, when he was 14 years old. In June of that year, his class took an end-of-term trip to the city of Gdansk on the Baltic coast. This was the first time that Lech had been away from Popowo and its neighboring villages. He remembered later that his first glimpse of the wide flat beach and the sea beyond left him with what he called "the memory of something vast, stretching out endlessly—possibly freedom."

Nine years later that memory would draw Lech Walesa back to Gdansk to make his mark on history.

4

The Worker's Life

POLES LIKE LECH Walesa, who grew up after World War II, were destined to become part of a new generation of industrial workers. The country's communist leaders were determined to transform Poland into a modern industrial state. The government established training and employment programs to draw young men to the nation's ports, mines, and industrial centers.

This appealed to Walesa, who had no desire to remain a rural peasant. He hoped to attend the government-run College of Technology, where he could receive an engineer's certificate—the key to a good job in postwar Poland and a passport out of Popowo. Walesa's school record was average, but his grades in mathematics and physics were good enough to get him a positive recommendation to the college. He passed the entrance exam, and then, to his great disappointment, learned that his family could not afford to pay the necessary fees. He was not to attend college after all.

Walesa was deeply discouraged by this setback. He went back to farm chores and brickmaking, wondering glumly if this was to be his future. But his mother urged him to consider other possibilities. His older brother Stanislaw had gone to Lipno, about 15 miles from Popowo, to attend a trade school. Although this vocational school was not as prestigious as the College of Technology, Feliksa Walesa correctly pointed out to her son that it would provide him with skills that would allow him to earn a livelihood without farming. So in September 1959, around the time he turned 16, Walesa set off for Lipno.

The trade school was designed to prepare young men to work for the state agricultural department (called the State Machinery Center or the POM, its initials in Polish) or in the industrial centers that were being created along the Baltic coast. Walesa enrolled in the school's agricultural mechanization division, where he would learn to do a mechanic's and electrician's work. The students took simple classes in academic subjects, such as Polish, math, history, and geography, but the school's real efforts went into their technical training. Walesa did not excel in the academic classes. Ironically, in view of the fact that he was destined to make Polish history, he did worst in history class.

"I didn't appreciate the value of history until much later," he now says. "It seemed to me remote from real life, an abstraction, describing people and facts devoid of the slightest link with reality as I knew it." Walesa did better in his workshop classes, where he had the chance to take apart and assemble many kinds of machinery, and in business management and gymnastics.

During his time in Lipno, Walesa lived with other students in a hostel, or students' rooming house. His conduct there was not perfect, and his record carried the notation "smokes and is a troublemaker." Walesa sometimes led his hostel-mates on forbidden excursions around town without the student caps they were supposed to wear at all times, and he often smoked cigarettes on the roof, which was also forbidden. Yet he proved to be a gifted organizer, and the authorities at the school and hostel could count on him to get things done. For example, he was good at leading other students in work crews assigned to sweep the floors or do other chores. Walesa's crew always got the job done ahead of schedule. During his two years at the trade school, Walesa returned to Popowo often during his free time to work on the family farm.

In 1961, Walesa graduated from the trade school with a certificate showing him to be a skilled worker. He attended a dance held to celebrate the end of school, and he recalls that the dance "marked the end of a life free from worries." Like many a student before and since, Walesa had come face-to-face with the reality of life after school: "Now I was going to have to work."

He got a job as an electrician with the POM at a place called Lochocino, not far from Popowo. He repaired electrical equipment and all sorts of machinery, and he was so good at it that people started calling him "the mechanic with golden hands."

Two years later, Walesa's work at the POM was interrupted when he was drafted into the army. At that time, all young Polish men were required to perform two years of military service. He served as a Morse code radio and telegraph operator, performed well, and was promoted to the rank of corporal. Walesa's commanding officer wrote in his file that Walesa was "intelligent, keen to learn" and "would make a leader." The path to a career in the army was open, but Walesa chose not to follow it. In 1965, when his service was over, he returned to work for the POM, this time in a place called Lenie, which was even closer to Popowo. He moved back into the family home.

The two years that followed were comfortable ones for Walesa. He was in his early twenties, and people in the community looked up to him because he had a good job. Although he was supposed to be working on the tractors and other machinery that belonged to the state, he spent a fair amount of his time on projects of his own. He worked his own small plot of land with equipment from the POM or used POM spare parts to repair friends' equipment. This was standard practice for POM mechanics and was tolerated by the supervisors, who realized that the small private farms of the region were much more important to the Polish economy than the few state-operated collectives.

Walesa was soon recognized as one of the top mechanics around Lenie. He learned to fix anything, from plows to washing machines, from motorbikes to television sets. He repaired appliances for friends and townspeople, who were always happy to give him a little money or a bottle of vodka in return for these favors. He was something of a dandy too, wearing work pants with a knife-sharp crease and a beret cocked at a jaunty angle. He remembers that people were always glad to see him at dances and parties, which made him feel important. "I was somebody," he said later. "It seemed I had found my place in life."

But Walesa was not satisfied for long. In May 1967, he suddenly felt disgusted with what he was doing. He was 23 years old, still living at home, and he wondered if he was wasting his life, coasting along on his reputation as a good mechanic. His comfortable little world seemed petty and unimportant. On top of everything else, a girl he had been dating broke up with him, and his pride was hurt. One afternoon he went home, got his coat and some money, and went to the train station. The next train to leave was going to Gdansk and Gdynia on the Baltic coast. Without hesitation, Walesa bought a ticket. He remembered his school trip of 1958, and the memory of that open expanse of sky, sea, and beach drew him like a magnet.

Walesa intended to go to Gdynia. But the train stopped first at Gdansk, and he got off to have a beer. He missed the train and decided to have a look around Gdansk while he waited for the next one. Almost at once he ran into a friend from the Lipno trade school. This friend told Walesa that he had been working at the shipyard in Gdansk for a few years, and he suggested that Walesa try to get a job there. So, abandoning his plan of going on to Gdynia, Walesa presented himself at the Lenin Shipyard on May 30, 1967, and filled out a job application. A few days later he was hired as a naval electrician at the shipyard. This was his introduction to the site where he would lead the 1980 strike.

Lenin Shipyard was an enormous place. More than 15,000 employees worked there: engineers, welders, painters, electricians, and others. They built huge steel tankers, commercial fishing vessels, and military ships. The shipyard was one of the biggest such operations in Poland, and the Polish government was very proud of it. Important foreign visitors and dignitaries who toured Poland were almost always required to make a visit to the Lenin Shipyard so that they could admire modern Polish industry at its finest.

As Walesa was to discover, though, the shipyard looked quite different to those who labored in it. Working conditions were deplorable. Workers put in ten-hour days, six days a week, working in the open air no matter what the weather. There were no lockers or clothes dryers, so that if a worker got soaked to the skin on the job, he had to wear his wet clothing home. The bathrooms and changing rooms did not meet the workers' needs.

"When I arrived," Walesa now says, "our shipyard looked like a factory filled with men in filthy rags, unable to wash themselves or urinate in toilets. You can't imagine how humiliating these working conditions were."

One thing that the yard did offer was job training in welding, mechanics, and other skills. Each year, between 8,000 and 9,000 employees attended these professional training courses. In addition, many young men who wanted to join the navy or the merchant marine found that a job at the shipyard often led to a career at sea.

Walesa's first days on the job were a bit of a shock. He says, "Although I had been a valued employee at the POM, I felt completely lost when I first started work at the shipyard in 1967." He became confused and disoriented the first time he climbed up inside the giant, unfinished hull of a ship, crisscrossed with scaffolding and decked with ladders. The whole experience of the yard was disorienting. After several years of being something of a big shot in the tiny village of Lenie, Walesa now found himself just another number—number 61-878 in fact—among thousands of other workers just like him. "A painful truth," he reflects, "but there was no going back."

One of the lessons he quickly learned was that the shipyard had a very complex caste system, or pecking order. Some jobs, such as engineering, had much higher status and pay than others, such as painting. Within each type of job, there was another system of rank, running from manager at the top, down through supervisor and foreman, to the workers who were at the bottom. Finally, workers who had held their positions for a long time and were considered permanent members of their work crews had more status than the lowly "temps," who were shuffled around from crew to crew. All of this made it a bit difficult for a young man from the country—a young man who had had a rather high opinion of himself—to find his way around in the society of the yard. Still, Walesa adjusted well. He was assigned to a work brigade that was installing electrical cables in large fishing boats. He soon mastered the tasks he was expected to perform and also made friends among his coworkers.

Housing was in desperately short supply in Poland at the end of the 1960s. According to Polish economist Wlodzimierz Brus, at that time a newly married couple had to wait an average of seven years before being assigned their own apartment. Only the higher-ranking shipyard workers, married people with families and some seniority, could manage to get apartments in Gdansk. The others, the young single men, had to make other arrangements. Walesa thought that the unluckiest of these were the 1,800 or so workers who lived in dormitories or hostels owned by the yard. For the most part, these were miserable, depressing places, with tiny rooms, broken furniture, and communal kitchens and showers. Some of the workers drank heavily, and the hostels often erupted in drunken brawls on the weekends.

Another 2,000 workers lived in rented rooms in private houses in the city. The shipyard paid their rent, but the roomers were expected to add a little money of their own to what their landlords received. Walesa was fortunate enough to live in a rented room—a small room that he shared with three other men for two years. The room had a table and four beds; its window

45

looked out onto a noisy streetcar route. Nevertheless, Walesa and his roommates considered themselves lucky to have such good living quarters. They liked their landlords, the Krol family, and they shared in household activities, such as mopping the floors, listening to the radio with Mr. Krol, and chaperoning the Krols' daughter at local dances.

At the same time, Walesa was involved in romances of his own. Soon after coming to Gdansk, he met a girl named Lala who dropped mysterious hints that she was the daughter of an important official. To impress her, Walesa spent more money than he could really afford on their dates, and he told her that he was the manager of a business. Their mutual game of deception ended early one morning when he saw Lala, muffled up in a shawl, delivering milk. He confessed that he was only an electrician at the shipyard, but neither of them wanted to see the other again.

Next Walesa dated a nurse who worked in a hospital near the yard. She was attractive and pleasant, but Walesa felt that something was missing from their relationship. He found that spark of excitement, though, in late 1968 when he saw a pretty, dark-eyed, dark-haired girl working in a flower shop. He could not get her out of his mind, so he went back to the shop and asked her out. Her name was Mirka Danuta Golos, but Walesa always called her Danuta, or Danka. Like Walesa, she was from the country, having arrived in Gdansk only recently. And she also came from a large family. Danuta was 19 years old when they met. Walesa was 25. Soon they were dating regularly, often going to movies together, and before long they decided to marry.

The marriage took place on November 8, 1969. Their wedding photograph shows a proud but nervous-looking groom, clean-shaven and dressed in a dark formal suit, and a bride in white with flowers and a lace veil, smiling serenely into the future.

Once he was married, Walesa had to find new living quarters. He and Danuta embarked on the frustrating odyssey of every newlywed couple in the cities of Po-land—trying to find a decent place to live. They wandered "from one inhospitable rented room to the next," as he describes it. For a time they lived in the married quarters of one of the shipyard hostels, but they fled those dreary surroundings as soon as possible. They rented a room in the attic over a small hairdressing shop on Beethoven Street. Although their quarters were tiny, they liked living there. In the summer they helped their landlady, the shop's owner, work in her small garden. Walesa, who had hated the thought of being a farmer, admits that after several years in the city he found himself "glad of the chance to get close to the soil." The couple's first child, a son they named Bogdan, was born in December 1970.

Courtship and marriage filled Walesa's personal life during the late 1960s, but he was also taking note of political events. The most dramatic of these events occurred in early 1968, before Walesa met Danuta, when Poland was shaken by a round of student protests.

The protests started when the government ordered the National Theater in Warsaw to shut down its production of a play called *Forefathers' Eve*, written by Adam Mickiewicz, a Polish poet of the nineteenth century who was honored by all Poles for his patriotic devotion to his homeland. The play is about Poland's fight against its Russian oppressors after the partitions in the eighteenth century when Poland vanished from the map of Europe. During the 1968 production in Warsaw, many audience members began cheering loudly at lines of dialogue that criticized the unjust rule of the Russian tyrants.

Fearful of offending their Soviet backers, Poland's communist leaders forced the play to close. This outraged the Polish people, who saw it as clear evidence that their government cared more about keeping the Soviets happy than about their cultural heritage. At the conclusion of the final performance, a group of angry university students marched from the theater to a statue of Mickiewicz in the center of town. The military police had been warned that the students were on their way, and a fight broke out. A number of students were beaten and jailed.

This incident was followed by an outbreak of unrest in March among Poland's students, professors, writers, and other intellectuals. Student-led demonstrations took place on university campuses and in the cities. In all, at least 2,000 Polish students were arrested and expelled from their schools. The Polish government, like all totalitarian regimes, could not accept the idea of what is sometimes called a loyal opposition—that is, people who are opposed to the government but loyal to the country. In democratic countries it is possible to criticize the government in power and still be considered a loyal citizen of the state. But in totalitarian countries like Poland in 1968, the government in power *is* the state. Any citizen who is not for the government is considered to be a disloyal traitor, and there is no middle ground. Protests and criticism cannot be tolerated.

Gomulka, Communist party secretary, acted quickly to crush the protests with force. He blamed the unrest and widespread disturbances on Poland's intellectual community. To prevent students and intellectuals from forming an alliance with the farm laborers and factory workers, who were increasingly unhappy about low wages and food shortages, the government sent representatives into the factories to get the workers angry at the students. These officials called the student protesters "hooligans" and "spoiled brats" and most of the workers agreed. They had no feeling of unity with the students. The students were talking about abstractions, such as freedom of speech and freedom of the press, while the workers were interested in the number of hours in a workday and whether there would be food on their dinner tables.

At the Lenin Shipyard, Walesa and a few others tried to persuade their coworkers to listen to what the students had to say. They suggested that perhaps the students and intellectuals were being treated as badly by the government as the workers were. But this "faint flicker of solidarity," as Walesa describes it, did not ignite a bonfire of fellowship between workers and intellectuals. All the same, Walesa began to realize that

49

the government was afraid of what might happen if all the different discontented groups—students, intellectuals, factory workers, farmers, clergy—ever joined together.

The student protests—and the government propaganda against the students—served to distract people's attention from economic problems for a while, but the economy was still in trouble. Life at the shipyard was affected. In an attempt to cut costs, the management of the yard told workers to work faster and harder—for the same amount of pay. Many workers, disgusted with their working conditions and with the way the shipyard was run, took to drinking on the job. They were searched for alcohol at the plant entrance, but they built stills in out-of-the-way places, such as the tops of construction cranes, and made their own alcohol inside the yard. The management continued to press for better productivity, without giving workers the tools and supplies they needed to do their jobs right. This haste and pressure led to the tragedy of the ship *Konopnicka.*

The yard missed its deadline to complete work on the *Konopnicka,* so 200 men were ordered to work around the clock until the ship was finished. The *Konopnicka*'s fuel tanks were filled before the work was done, and a spark from a welder's torch ignited gas that had leaked from a faulty pipe. A huge explosion tore at the inside of the vessel and fires broke out. Men were trapped inside the burning hull, but the hatchways in the hull had been sealed during construction.

50

They could not get out, and it was impossible to get firefighting gear in to them.

Outside the burning ship, desperate workers tried to cut through the hull with torches to rescue their trapped colleagues, but the supply of fuel for the torches ran out. Twenty-two men perished in the *Konopnicka*. To the shipyard workers, the tragedy of the *Konopnicka* was a symbol of how uncaring the system was. However, worse was soon to come.

5

Poles Against Poles

PARTY SECRETARY GOMULKA never forgot that the person who had held that post before him, Boleslaw Bierut, had been driven out of office by the Poznan worker riots of 1956, and that those riots had been caused, at least in part, by high food prices. Throughout the 1960s, therefore, Gomulka's government managed to keep food prices fairly steady. But as the decade drew to a close, food shortages became more and more of a problem. Prices at the state-owned stores were low, because those prices were set by the government, which wanted to avoid price riots, but the stores often had little or nothing to sell. Much more food was available on the black market, from farmers and butchers who illegally sold their food directly to the public. But black market prices were higher. Poles therefore spent a great deal of time shopping, trying to find a place to get what they needed at a price they could afford, and then standing in line, often for hours, to get it.

In December 1970, Gomulka decided that he had to

raise food prices. On Saturday, December 12, the government announced that the prices of basic goods, such as jam, pork, flour, fish, and sugar, would go up by anywhere from 12 to 36 percent. Clothing prices were also raised.

The price increases could not have come at a worse time. It was a couple of weeks before Christmas—the time when Polish shoppers traditionally stock their cupboards for holiday meals and buy gifts of clothing for their families. The announcement was met with stunned outrage.

Two days later, on Monday, December 14, workers in Gdansk, Gdynia, and Szczecin—all industrial cities on the Baltic coast—went on strike. A thousand workers streamed out of the gates of the Lenin Shipyard to tell the authorities that they would not go along with the price increases.

They marched to the headquarters of the district committee of the PZPR, and there they overturned a loudspeaker car that belonged to the party. Then the strikers went to the engineering school. They apologized to the students for having ignored their pleas for unity in 1968, and they asked the students to join the strike. But Poland's intellectuals and students were not ready to trust the workers so soon after the rejection of 1968, and the students ignored the call. By this time, however, the militia had caught up with the strikers. Fighting broke out in the streets. People were injured, and quite a few strikers were arrested.

Walesa was not present when the strikes broke out because his work brigade had that day off. He reported to the yard at 6:30 the next morning, December 15. The supervisor of his workshop was trying to persuade the workers to stay at their posts, but a parade of strikers went by on their way to the office of the yard's director, a man named Zaczek. Walesa and the others from his workshop joined this group. They stood outside Zaczek's window, chanting their demands: stable food prices, better pay, and the release of workers who had been arrested the day before. Zaczek could do nothing for them, so the workers set off for the Communist party headquarters in town.

Excited that action was being taken at last, Walesa pushed his way to the very front of the crowd of marchers. But as he approached the gate he saw that thirty or more police waited outside, waving their nightsticks in a menacing manner. He hesitated for a moment, sure that they would be attacked. Then, he recalls, "I felt something like a great gasp of exhaled breath blowing from the crowd at my back; incredible as it may seem, I felt that breath physically and it was as if I was carried forward by it." Uplifted and inspired by the crowd's support, Walesa boldly led the strikers in a rush through the police line.

When they reached PZPR headquarters, the workers found the place deserted, except for a few guards armed with machine guns. They moved on to the militia post where the people who had been arrested the previous day were being held. There, the strike got out of control.

Walesa went into the commander's office and asked

him to release the workers who were being held. The commander was willing to do this, but the mass of strikers in the courtyard now took matters into their own hands, seizing stones and sticks as if for an attack. Just then, militia deputies from other parts of the post, not knowing what was going on in the commander's office, poured into the courtyard with drawn guns. At that moment, Walesa appeared in the window of the commander's office. He intended to announce that the prisoners would be freed and to ask for help in identifying them, but the workers below, seeing him safe in the office while they were surrounded by angry militia personnel, began hurling stones at him and calling him a traitor. While the workers were yelling that Walesa was a double agent and a police spy, the militia started throwing smoke bombs. Soon no one could be sure what was going on. The strike had lost all order and direction. Walesa sneaked out of the building and escaped through back alleys. He was demoralized and dismayed. He had felt such a bond of fellowship with the other workers back at the shipyard gate. He had thought that they could get the jailed workers freed from the militia prison under his leadership. Now everything had gone wrong, all because of hasty judgments and nervous overreactions on both sides. And worst of all, Walesa wondered, would the other workers trust him again?

While Walesa was slipping away from the militia headquarters toward his apartment, a militia officer panicked and shot a shipyard worker who was blocking his way in a city street. A crowd of enraged workers seized and killed him. Already the strike had brought violent death to both sides.

That afternoon the army sent two tanks to the shipyard to restore order. The workers captured the tanks by sticking mud in the viewing slits and then waiting for the blinded drivers to emerge. The tanks were taken to Gate Number 2 of the shipyard and proudly displayed like trophies of war.

Walesa ventured out again in the afternoon. On his way to the shipyard he met several coworkers. One ran away from him in fear. The other warned him not to go to the yard. Walesa went ahead anyway, noticing as he went that some shops had been broken into. People were beginning to drink and loot. Walesa feared that a murderous riot could erupt at any moment.

At the shipyard, he found that the other workers had forgotten or forgiven his role in the fiasco at the militia station. In fact, the people in his workshop chose him as their delegate to the strike committee that was being formed, and then he was chosen as head of the three-person committee. But because his faith in his own leadership abilities had been shaken by the morning's disaster at the militia post, Walesa refused to act as the committee's president. He declared that the three members would share responsibility equally. As it turned out, the committee had little real effect on the course of the strike. Walesa later felt that the committee was too indecisive and uncertain. He was left believing that if he had been willing to take the risk and act as a single strong leader, the strike committee might have been more effective.

Some strikers went home that night. Others remained in the yard. Walesa was one of the ones who stayed. He tried to snatch a few hours' sleep curled up on the floor on a pile of old coats. The next morning, December 16, all the striking workers assembled at the yard. Then they learned that army troops and tanks had surrounded the yard, blocking the gates and cutting off access to nearby streets and roads.

Walesa went with the other members of the strike committee to the office of the director. They asked Zaczek to telephone army headquarters and negotiate for the withdrawal of the troops. Zaczek claimed that he could not get through to the authorities, and Walesa and the others left his office. No one was sure what to do next. Suddenly, however, matters were taken out of their hands. The sound of gunfire ripped through the air near Gate Number 2. At first Walesa thought that soldiers were firing blanks to frighten the workers. Then more gunshots sounded, and he saw workers scrambling to flee, screaming in terror. Several fell. When the shooting stopped, three workers lay dead. One was from Walesa's workshop. A fourth worker died on his way to the hospital.

Shocked and horrified, the shipyard workers quickly organized a sort of memorial, draping the dead workers' helmets with black cloth and holding them aloft. Massed at the gate, the workers sang Poland's national anthem, which is called "Poland Has Not Perished."

When they came to the words "We'll recover with the sword what the enemy forces have taken from us," they sang extra loudly, and they followed the anthem with a chant of "Murderers! Murderers!" aimed at the soldiers outside the gate.

With four dead, the strike was finished. The workers agreed to leave the yard. Thousands of them filed out between rows of armed soldiers. Walesa was one of them, and as he headed for home, he was aware that he was being followed by the secret police (the SB). That night two men from the SB came to the Walesas' apartment and took him away. Danuta recalls that before they left, her husband handed her his watch and wedding ring, telling her to sell them if she needed money. Then he was gone.

The SB released Walesa a few days later. He had been interrogated. He told the SB that the workers would continue to demand better conditions and the right to strike. But, he admits, "I didn't leave with my hands entirely clean." Before the SB would release Walesa, he had to sign a *lojalka,* or certificate of loyalty to the state. All labor activists or political opposition-ists who were arrested had to sign these certificates. Those who refused as a matter of principle were likely to spend a long time in jail. Walesa signed because he felt he owed it to his family to get out of the hands of the police.

Violent protests took place in other Polish cities besides Gdansk. Government authorities claimed that 45 people were killed and nearly 1,000 injured in the

December 1970 disturbances. In addition, many workers were arrested. Walesa was one of many Poles who believed that it was vital to keep the people's memory of that December alive. He was determined to someday build a monument in honor of the workers who had been killed at Gate Number 2.

Though tragic, the workers' protests of 1970 did achieve one result. Like the Poznan riots in 1956, they toppled the party secretary from power. Gomulka was replaced by Edward Gierek, a former coal miner from the mining region of Silesia in southern Poland. One of Gierek's first moves was to meet with workers' representatives in Warsaw in January 1971. Walesa was elected to represent his workshop at this meeting. Later Gierek came to the shipyard and made a moving, emotional appeal to the workers there. He ended by asking them, "Will you help me?"

The workers responded with enthusiastic applause and called out, "We will help you." Walesa shared their enthusiasm. He believed that Gierek, who had once been a laborer himself, would improve things for the working-class people of Poland.

The workers at the shipyard had a trade union at this time, as did all Polish factories, but these factory unions belonged to the government's Central Council of the Trade Unions (CRZZ in Polish). They were sponsored by the state and infiltrated by government representatives from the PZPR. The chairman of the Central Council of the Trade Unions was a high-ranking member of the Communist party. The unions never disagreed with party directives, and top union officials used their influence to get workers to vote for the party's favorite candidates.

In the first surge of optimism after Gierek came to power, Walesa thought that the state-run trade union might be allowed to function as a truly free union, with the rights to strike, to criticize government policies, and to negotiate with shipyard management. Walesa's coworkers elected him to the post of inspector for the union. He liked working as an inspector because it allowed him to visit all parts of the shipyard, to talk to employees in every workshop, and to listen to their complaints and problems. But before long he realized that the state-sponsored trade union was still a sham. The shipyard managers did not consult the union about important decisions, and they did not negotiate wages and working conditions with it. In 1972, Walesa refused to stand for reelection to the post of union inspector.

Meanwhile, Gierek had launched an ambitious plan of economic reform designed to increase Polish prosperity. Gierek's plan relied on borrowing large sums from the Soviet Union and from Western nations. But after borrowing the money, Poland failed to earn enough to repay its foreign loans and sank deeper into debt. Once again, there were shortages of goods such as food, clothing, and shoes.

Wages had been increasing, however, although most workers found their work hours increased at the same time. Walesa reports that by 1973 many workers had to get up at four or five o'clock in the morning to get to

60

work on time and did not leave their jobs until eight o'clock at night. Working conditions remained uncomfortable and dangerous. "Anyone who doesn't know what is meant by the expression 'rat-men' should come to the shipyard," Walesa says, "and see how the men crawl on their stomachs with their rust scrubbers inside long pipes just wide enough for a man's body, covered in rust and sweat, or how they creep, armed with their acetylene blowtorches, to work under the tankers' petroleum tanks. Then they'll see what's meant by exhausting, inhuman labor that ruins a man's health."

As time went on, Walesa became more and more convinced that the workers needed an independent union, free from Communist party influence, to protect their rights.

Around the same time, Walesa faced a personal crisis. His mother and stepfather were planning to move to the United States. Feliksa Walesa very much wanted Lech and his wife and children to accompany them, but Lech refused. "I shall never leave Poland," he told his mother. "We have to try and make Poland work." Walesa never saw his mother again. In 1975 she was killed in an auto accident in the United States.

By the mid-1970s, it was clear that Gierek's economic reform program was failing. As always, the economic climate affected the Lenin Shipyard. Profits fell, and the yard's managers began lowering workers' wages.

In February 1976, Walesa made a passionate speech at a meeting of the shipyard's official union. He de-

61

clared that Gierek had betrayed and lied to the workers of Poland, and that the workers needed a trade union to speak for them. He wanted to be elected to the CRZZ—perhaps he could accomplish something as a member of the central council.

Walesa's speech was well received by the shipyard workers, but not so well received by management and the local PZPR committee. He was summoned to the director's office, where several secret police were waiting for him. If he was elected, they asked, would he be prepared to cooperate and say what they told him to say? Walesa said he would not, and with no more ado he was seized by the elbows and hustled out of the shipyard. He was placed on suspension and two months later he was fired.

The summer of 1976 brought more labor unrest to Poland. In June, Gierek's government announced steep increases in food prices. The next day, strikes and antigovernment demonstrations broke out everywhere. The government backed down, canceling the price increases, but many workers were beaten by the police and militia, fired from their jobs, or arrested. But this time, the unrest brought the workers and intellectuals of Poland together. The workers facing trial did not have money for lawyers, and a group of intellectuals who opposed the government formed a committee to raise money for them. This Workers' Defense Committee (called KOR for its Polish initials) not only paid legal fees but also gave food and money to the families of the jailed workers. Some of the organizers of the

KOR were veterans of the 1968 student protests. Chief among them were Jacek Kuron and Adam Michnik, both of whom had spent time in jail for criticizing the government.

With KOR's encouragement, oppositionist writers and artists began producing underground newsletters—published without being submitted to the government censors for approval. These sheets were furtively printed on stencil machines in people's apartments and passed from hand to hand. They contained articles, poetry, and drawings that criticized or made fun of the government, and they also contained essays and debates about the plight of the workers.

This was the beginning of cooperation among the various opposition groups in Poland. KOR was broadened and named the Committee for Social Self-Defence-KOR, or KSS-KOR. Another group, the Catholic church, joined the opposition force as well. Stefan Cardinal Wyszynski, head of the Polish church, spoke out boldly about the government's responsibility to treat workers fairly, and he encouraged other clergy to do the same.

While all of this was going on, Walesa was working at a company called ZREMB in the Stogi section of Gdansk, where he and his family now lived. He had been hired in May 1976 to repair vehicles. The job gave him the opportunity to patch up an old abandoned car and take the family for a visit to Danuta's home village. He also made a little extra money by doing repair jobs for friends on the side, just as he had done in the old days while working for the POM. But although he had been expelled from the shipyard, Walesa had not lost his interest in politics.

In 1977, after the KOR got started, he began hearing about oppositionist activities. In 1978 he started seeing copies of the *Coastal Worker,* an underground newsletter published by the opposition. He learned of a group called the Young Poland Movement (RMP in Polish), a student organization dedicated to commemorating events in the Polish struggle for independence, including the December 1970 shootings at the Lenin Shipyard. Each December 16, RMP members placed wreaths outside Gate Number 2 to honor the workers who had been killed there. They were always arrested for doing this.

Next Walesa learned that a handful of workers led by Andrzej Gwiazda, an electrical engineer, had founded something they called the Free Trades Unions commission (WZZ in Polish). He read about it in the *Coastal Worker,* and saw with surprise that Gwiazda and the others had included their names and even their addresses. He got in touch with them and learned that the WZZ was intended to be an independent, self-governing trade union, one that would represent workers freely and honestly. Soon he was part of a core group of WZZ planners that included Gwiazda and his wife, Joanna, a young worker named Bogdan Lis, Anna Walentynowicz from the Lenin Shipyard, and a nurse named Alina Pienkowska, also from the shipyard. The WZZ was closely tied to both the KOR and the RMP, and the students, intellectuals, and workers in the various groups soon got to know one another.

Never content to sit on the sidelines, Walesa quickly got involved in oppositionist work—for example, passing out copies of the *Coastal Worker* to people riding on streetcars or leaving church. Andrzej Gwiazda remembers that the first time he and Walesa distributed the newsletter together, Walesa was so nervous that his hands shook. A little nervousness was natural. Both the WZZ and the newsletter were illegal, and Gwiazda and Walesa could have been arrested. Later Walesa organized a Free Trades Unions group in his own Stogi neighborhood and wrote a pamphlet describing the December 1970 strike. He was arrested several times as an oppositionist, and in November of 1978 he was fired from ZREMB for criticizing that company's branch of the state-run trade union.

Walesa remained unemployed for three months. Every day he signed in at the government employment office and went out on a job interview. But instead of trying to get the job, he would pass out copies of the *Coastal Worker* and other WZZ materials. Finally, on the last day of his three months of unemployment benefits, he took a job at the Elektromontaz engineering firm. However, his stint there was even shorter than his time at ZREMB. In December 1979, the ninth anniversary of the 1970 strike, Walesa took part in a memorial service at Gate Number 2 of the shipyard.

Still dreaming of the day when there would be a monument to the fallen workers, he climbed up on the wall and said to the 7,000 people who had gathered there, "Next year on the tenth anniversary, each of you

65

must bring a stone or brick to this spot. We shall cement them into place and we shall build a monument." The militia stood by but did not interfere, perhaps because the crowd was so large, or perhaps because—for the first time—it included priests, who led prayers for the dead.

This speech made Walesa something of a local hero in Stogi. When the police came to arrest him, his neighbors threw shoes, hot water, and garbage at them from the upper windows. But Walesa's outspoken oppositionism did not make him popular with the managers of Elektromontaz, who promptly fired him. Out of work and out of money, Walesa turned to the KOR, which provided food for his family and a lawyer for his appearances in court.

Workers, students, dissident writers, and liberal priests were all tired of the Gierek government. The promised improvements in the economy had failed to materialize, and police persecution was increasing. On July 1, 1980, when the government raised meat prices, workers in Lublin went on strike. This time they demanded not just economic benefits but political and social reform as well. In addition to stable food prices and better pay, they called for a free press and free trade unions.

Other strikes were called across Poland, including some at small factories in Gdansk. The workers at the Lenin Shipyard shared the general unrest. Then, in August, the shipyard fired Anna Walentynowicz and the WZZ called for a strike. The curtain rose on the great drama of Solidarity, with Lech Walesa at center stage.

6

"We Shall Not Yield"

WALESA WAS JUST one of many opposition-ists in the Gdansk area who believed that the firing of Anna Walentynowicz, along with bad working conditions and the economic problems that affected all Poles, were good reasons for a strike at the shipyard. Yet as he rode the rattling streetcar toward the shipyard on August 14, 1980, Walesa wondered whether the workers were somehow being manipulated by the authorities.

"I knew I was being followed by the secret police," he explained later. "I could see their unmarked car following behind. What if this strike was just what they wanted? What exactly were they plotting? And were the authorities counting on us to show our hand so as to be able to gun us down, the lot of us?" A high-ranking party official had recently announced that the authorities knew the names and addresses of 12,000 oppositionists in Gdansk. "It would take only a matter of hours to put us all behind bars," Walesa explains. Yet he stayed on the streetcar until it arrived at the shipyard. Then he scaled the wall and leaped onto the bulldozer to interrupt Gniech, the yard's director.

After Walesa's fiery speech, the workers voted overwhelmingly to continue the strike. They also voted to make him the head of the strike committee. Walesa wanted no repetition of the violence that had occurred in 1970 when the strikers went out into the streets, so he declared that this strike would be an occupation strike—the striking workers would remain inside the yard until it was settled. And this time they would not give up until their demands were met.

At first the workers had four demands: the reinstatement of Anna Walentynowicz and Lech Walesa in their jobs at the yard, a promise of no punishment for the strikers, a monument built to the victims of the 1970 strike, and a pay raise for each worker. Walesa and the committee met with Director Gniech in the Health and Safety hall of the yard. The strike committee insisted on having the meeting broadcast to the whole shipyard over the yard's radio station. That way, no deals would be made behind closed doors.

Gniech started by refusing to build a monument. Then he addressed the issue of pay raises. Walesa said that every worker's pay must be increased by the same amount. Gniech protested that the senior and more skilled workers should receive larger raises than the lower-level workers. Walesa and the committee disagreed. All the workers had to get the same amount. At this point, Gniech backed off on the issue of raises but agreed to have the monument built. Walesa was so jubilant that he seized the microphone and told the

68

strikers that the strike was working.

However, on the next day, August 15, things did not go so smoothly. The workers' families had gathered outside the shipyard walls to pray and to talk to the workers inside, many of whom wanted the strike to end so they could go home. The government had cut all the telephone lines to Gdansk, hoping to keep news of the strike from spreading to other cities. Director Gniech claimed that he was unable to contact the higher authorities and that he could not agree to the strikers' terms on his own. At the same time, a huge crowd was assembling outside the shipyard, curious to see what the outcome would be. The public transport system of Gdansk was shut down by the authorities, who hoped to keep people away from the shipyard, but onlookers and supporters continued to arrive on foot. An air of expectancy was building.

That same day, many more strikes started in the Baltic region. Perhaps workers were inspired because August 15 is a very special day in Poland. In the Roman Catholic calendar it is a holiday called the Feast of the Assumption, and in Poland it is also devoted to the Black Madonna of Czestochowa, an ancient portrait of the Virgin Mary that is Poland's most revered religious object. The Miracle on the Vistula, Marshal Pilsudski's heroic victory over the Soviets in 1920, took place on August 15 as well. Whatever the reason, strikes were called that day in scores of Polish factories, universities, and workshops.

The next day, however, the strikers were becoming discouraged. Many of them felt that they were not getting anywhere. Then Gniech offered to rehire Walenty-nowicz and Walesa and to give all shipyard workers an increase of 75 percent of what the strike committee had demanded. This offer provoked a crisis in Walesa's leadership.

Walesa and the rest of the strike committee agreed to accept Gniech's offer. Walesa took up the microphone and announced, "It's over! We've won!" The workers, who had been waiting impatiently for some kind of conclusion, sang the national anthem and then began leaving the yard. At this point trouble broke out. Workers from other factories, many of them on strike themselves and who had been watching the shipyard strike with their families, wanted the shipyard strikers to drive a harder bargain to serve as an example for their own strikes.

Influenced by the ideas of the WZZ, many people in the crowd hoped that the shipyard strike would bring about social and political reforms like those that had been demanded in Lublin. When, instead, the shipyard strikers accepted a reduced pay hike and went home, the onlookers felt betrayed. They began shouting at Walesa, calling him a traitor for knuckling under to management.

One of the angriest groups was made up of transport workers, the mechanics and drivers of Gdansk's streetcars and buses. One of them managed to get to a microphone and make a speech, pleading with the shipyard employees to support their fellow workers in other strikes, not just in Gdansk but all over the country. He was surrounded by several hundred young men who shouted their support.

"If you abandon us, we'll be lost!" another transport worker yelled at Walesa. Walesa realized that this crowd of disappointed workers was not about to offer him a polite greeting if he tried to leave the yard. He also realized that the strike committee had given in too easily, and that all the workers of Gdansk—perhaps all the workers of Poland—wanted someone to lead them in a unified action. Perhaps this strike could win the workers more than a few small concessions about jobs and wages. Perhaps it was time to demand what the WZZ had been talking about for several years: free trade unions, freedom of speech for all, and worker participation in economic planning.

Walesa jumped onto a small electric cart, rode to Gate Number 2, and called out through a microphone, "If you want to go on with the strike, it will go on! Who wants to go on?"

"We do!" roared the waiting crowd.

"Who doesn't want to go on with the strike?" he asked.

There was no response.

"So," Walesa said, "the strike goes on!"

The shipyard gates were closed. At the time only about 1,000 yard workers remained, but in the following days many returned. Other supporters also joined the group inside the yard. At its largest, the crowd of strikers numbered about 10,000.

In his 1987 autobiography, *A Way of Hope*, Walesa

wrote, "Solidarity was born at that precise moment when the shipyard strike evolved from a local success in the shipyard to a strike in support of other factories and business enterprises, large and small, in need of our protection: moral reasons impelled us toward solidarity with our neighbors and coworkers in every line of endeavor."

There were practical reasons as well. Walesa and his co-oppositionists believed that if they all spoke and acted as one, they would accomplish more. But not even Walesa knew how far down the road of change he was about to lead his fellow citizens.

Ironically, it was Gniech, the yard's director, who coined the name *Solidarity* for the movement. From his office, he heard the shouts of the crowd outside, and when Walesa returned to tell him that the strike was not over after all, Gniech said, "Well then, it isn't up to me anymore. It's not a shipyard strike anymore. It's a strike in solidarity."

Walesa and others seized on the word and made it their rallying cry. Two unemployed graphic artists in Gdansk designed a logo. It consisted of the word *Solidarność* in bold red letters, each letter touching and supporting the next, with the red-and-white flag of Poland streaming above.

All at once the strike at the Gdansk shipyard was a national and international event. In spite of the government's efforts to clamp down on information, the news spread throughout the country and around the world. Newspaper headlines and television broadcasts focused on the band of strikers who were holding Po-

72

land's communist government at bay—and on the strike's charismatic leader, Lech Walesa. Each day, people around the world checked the news for the latest developments, and almost overnight Walesa became a public figure, a hero whose name was synonymous with freedom and courage.

Meanwhile, inside the yard the strike entered its second phase—its Solidarity phase. A new strike committee was elected. It included WZZ members such as Bogdan Lis and Andrzej and Joanna Gwiazda, as well as Walesa and Walentynowicz. The committee drew up a new list of twenty-one demands, including economic reforms and protection for human and civil rights. Among other things, they demanded freedom of speech, an end to censorship of the press, and the freeing of all prisoners who had been jailed for oppositionist activities. They insisted that workers' groups be included in the government's economic planning and that managers of factories and workshops should get those positions on the basis of skill and knowledge, not as a reward for being loyal to the party. But the most important demand was that Polish workers be permitted to form free trade unions governed by workers' councils that would not be dominated by the Communist party or by factory management, unions that would be guaranteed the right to strike. Lists of the demands were handed out to the strikers and their supporters, and before long graffiti reading "21 × TAK" (21 times YES) appeared on walls everywhere.

Such demands, of course, were far beyond the power

of Klemens Gniech to negotiate. The workers waited for the government to send someone to meet with them. In the meanwhile, they formed a new organization, the Interfactory Strike Committee (MKS in Polish), headed by Walesa. This committee included representatives from other striking plants in Gdansk and elsewhere in Poland (by now more than 250 factories were on strike). The MKS wanted the strikers to behave in a disciplined manner, so it banned alcohol from the yard. Family members and well-wishers kept the strikers provided with bundles of food that were passed over the wall or through the gate, but each bundle was searched to make sure it did not contain a bottle of vodka. There was some grumbling, but most of the workers cheerfully agreed to the MKS rules.

Because the Lenin Shipyard strike was an occupation strike, not a work stoppage, work continued as usual in the workshops. There were a few differences, however. Gneich's orders were disregarded. The director spent the entire strike in his office, gazing glumly out his window at a shipyard he no longer controlled. Instead of going home at the end of the day, the workers ate their meals in the "strike kitchen," and then chatted with their coworkers or talked across the walls to their families before going to sleep in a workshop or in the courtyard. Members of the Young Poland Movement (RMP) played guitars and sang folk songs. Music alternated with strike announcements over the loudspeaker system (the Beatles' "Yellow Submarine" was a favorite of the strikers). One visiting journalist noted that although the purpose of the strike was deeply

74

serious, the place had something of "a carnival air." It also had a distinctly religious air. The strikers often prayed together. Gate Number 2 had been decorated with flowers, ribbons, crucifixes, and a large photograph of Pope John Paul II. Each afternoon, Mass was celebrated in front of the gate by Father Henryk Jankowski, a priest who had joined the strikers. Jankowski became a close friend and adviser to Walesa. The priest gave Walesa a small pin bearing the image of the Black Madonna of Czestochowa, and Walesa wore it on the lapel of his jacket every day.

The daily Mass was broadcast over the shipyard radio station, and it was followed by a daily address from Walesa, who clambered up onto the fence each evening to address the assembled strikers and onlookers. These speeches established Walesa's hold on his listeners. He spoke eloquently but simply, using homely phrases and examples that everyone understood, in a voice filled with sincerity. He felt that he had truly come into his own as a speaker.

"For the first time," he recalls, "my words were entirely in step with my thoughts and with the plan that I was trying to communicate to my audience." His confidence soared. "I really felt, however arrogant it might sound," he says, "that if anything was to be achieved, it was up to me to achieve it."

Walesa's belief in the force of his own leadership doubtless gave him the inner strength to keep going during the strike, but it also began to grate on other activists and members of the strike committee. Some of them started to feel that Walesa might be taking too much control of the movement into his own hands, or that he was getting too much of the limelight, letting the world think of him as Solidarity's sole leader, not just a spokesperson for the various opposition groups that were involved. A split between Walesa and some of his fellow organizers began at this time. At first it was so small as to be almost invisible, but it widened as later events unfolded.

On August 23, Deputy Prime Minister Mieczyslaw Jagielski arrived from Warsaw to negotiate with the strikers. Now the pressure was on Walesa. Could he really get the twenty-one demands accepted? He called in a group of liberal Polish intellectuals—writers, historians, economists, and theologians—to act as his advisers. This move angered some of the worker activists, who felt that they were losing control of the strike they had started; but Walesa thought it was important to hear differing points of view about negotiations that could well change the face of Poland.

The MKS committee met with Jagielski and his delegation inside the shipyard's conference hall. One wall was glass, and the striking workers were free to look into the hall and watch the proceedings. Some of them took advantage of this opportunity to make faces at Jagielski. The discussions were broadcast to the yard over the loudspeakers.

At first, Jagielski rejected almost all of the workers' demands. Over the next few days, however, he gradually came around and agreed with most of them. One stumbling block was that some of the KOR (Workers' Defense Committee) activists, including founders

Jacek Kuron and Adam Michnik, had been arrested during the strike, and there was confusion among the MKS committee delegates about whether an agreement should be signed before they were freed. Walesa felt that the negotiating team should stick to the original demands and try to get the prisoners released after the strike was settled, but not everyone shared this view. Some of the delegates were also put off by the way Walesa interrupted them or shouted them down when they disagreed with him.

But the real sticking point in the negotiations involved the issue of free trade unions. The government was not prepared to permit independent trade unions. They argued that under the communist system the party was the sole representative of the workers, so the existing state-run trade unions were the only unions they could allow. Walesa and the others insisted that independent unions, free from all outside domination, were the only unions they would accept.

Jagielski asked to speak with Walesa on this issue. Walesa agreed, and together with Adam Gwiazda, Bogdan Lis, and a few other advisers, he met with Jagielski in a closed room with no microphone. After several days of arguing, the two parties agreed that workers could form independent unions if the unions acknowledged that the Communist party had "a leading role in the state." That way, the new unions would not be under the official control of the party or the government, but they would recognize that the party still ruled Poland.

The MKS committee was fairly satisfied with this,

The strike is over! Lech Walesa raises his arms in victory, on August 30, 1980. The communist government's recognition of Solidarity as an independent trade union raised the hopes of Polish workers for more freedom and a better standard of living. JORMA PUUSA-LEHTI KUVA/PHOTORE-PORTERS but felt that Walesa had let them down by conducting the most important part of the negotiations behind closed doors. To many committee members, this was a violation of the open, democratic spirit of the strike. These committee members wanted to put the "leading role" proposal to a vote by all the strikers at the shipyard and elsewhere. An argument broke out in the conference hall, but Walesa ended the debate by starting to sing the national anthem. The delegates joined in, and the moment of disagreement passed. The MKS committee and the government team had agreed on the workers' demands.

Two days later, in a historic public ceremony that was witnessed by every Pole who could get to a television set, and by millions of people around the world, Walesa and Jagielski signed the Gdansk Agreement, which gave Polish workers the right to form independent trade unions and to strike. This was the first time that such freedoms had been granted to workers in any country that was part of the Soviet bloc of nations.

At the ceremony, Walesa spoke to the workers. "We have fought, not for ourselves nor for our own interests, but for the entire country," he told them. "We have fought for all of you. And now, with the same determination and solidarity that we showed on strike, we shall go back to work. As of tomorrow, the new life of our trade union begins. Let us take care that it remains independent and self-governing, working for us all and for the good of Poland. I proclaim that the strike is over."

With that, Lech Walesa was carried out of the shipyard on the shoulders of cheering workers.

7

Solidarity

THE STRIKE WAS over, but a new union called
Solidarity had just been born. Walesa had expected to go back to his old job as an electrician
at the shipyard, but he soon discovered that running
the union was full-time work.

Walesa was appointed to serve as acting chairman
until the union could organize a national meeting to
elect officers. He needed an office, so he arranged for
the use of an apartment until a proper headquarters
could be found. When he showed up to open the office,
carrying a wreath of flowers from Danuta under one
arm and a wooden crucifix for the wall under the other,
he was greeted by a crowd of reporters who clamored
to know what Solidarity would do next.

"I am not interested in politics," Walesa told them. "I
am a union man. My job now is to organize the union."
And although Walesa tried to do just that, he was to
learn that the union could not be separated from politics that easily.

Workers came from all over Poland, seeking his advice and help. Thousands joined Solidarity every day. Before long, the union had 10 million members, about 28 percent of the Polish population. At the same time, membership in the Workers' Party (PZRP), the official communist organization, dropped. Nearly a million Poles left the Communist party after the August strike, leaving it to represent only 7 percent of the population.

Walesa's office was deluged by the paperwork connected with all the new members and the formation of 38 regional chapters of the union. Countless hours were spent waiting to see how and when the government would put the Gdansk Agreement into practice. The terms of the agreement were very general, so it wasn't clear how constitutional law and everyday affairs would be affected. There were endless debates, conferences, speeches, telephone calls, arguments, ceremonial appearances, and other similar demands on Walesa's time.

The Solidarity offices were soon moved to a suite of rooms on two floors of the Hotel Morski in Gdansk. Walesa's salary was fixed at an amount equal to about $700 in U.S. currency each month, roughly three times the Polish national average. It was paid out of money collected as union dues—1 percent of each member's annual salary. Because Walesa hates to fly, he acquired a car and hired a driver to take him to the meetings and rallies he was expected to attend around the country.

Not long after the strike, the government assigned Walesa and Danuta a new six-room, three-bathroom apartment. The Walesas' new life-style earned them some criticism. Danuta reported that women in the neighborhood walked by the apartment frequently, "just to see how often we change the curtains." Some felt that Walesa should not have accepted a special favor from the state, but he pointed out that he and Danuta had requested the apartment years ago and had waited for it like everyone else.

Yet neither Walesa nor the other Solidarity leaders were quite sure just what sort of enterprise they had undertaken. A few years later, in 1987, Walesa revealed that he had often felt that the strike of August 1980 had happened before he and the other oppositionists were ready. "I was haunted," he wrote, "by the feeling that August had come too soon, that we needed a year or two more of hard work to prepare. . . . The declaration of the existence of independent trade unions implied that we had already worked out rules and guidelines for members to follow in order to avoid basic errors of our own management. But events had overtaken us; we no longer had any choice but to go on."

In truth, Solidarity's success in Gdansk had been so dramatic and unexpected that the oppositionists did not have a clear set of goals or, even more important, an administrative structure designed to help them reach those goals. Solidarity had two identities: it was a labor union, and it was also a broader social and political movement, perhaps the germ of a political party.

Some Solidarity members, like Walesa, tried to focus on the functions of the union, which were intended to

83

be much like those of unions everywhere. It was supposed to act on behalf of employees in negotiating wages and benefits, help employees resolve problems on the job or grievances against management, and generally represent the workers' point of view to management. But many people within Solidarity felt that the union had a responsibility to remain committed to a wider program of political reform. As the months passed, there would be profound differences of opinion on these issues.

In the fall of 1981 and the spring of 1982, however, a wave of optimism and excitement surged through Poland. The Poles called this lighthearted, hopeful spirit *odnowa*, or "renewal," and it was most noticeable in the new openness that filled Polish life. Students, journalists, and workers openly criticized the government and discussed Poland's economic problems. The Catholic church received permission to broadcast Sunday Mass on the radio, something it had been trying to do for decades. Reporters and photographers went more or less where they pleased in the country. A new passport law loosened travel restrictions, allowing Poles who could afford it to travel to other countries without hindrance. Theaters and television stations presented patriotic, anti-Russian works. A movie called *Man of Iron* by Andrzej Wajda told the story of the Gdansk shipyard strike, with Walesa himself in a cameo appearance, and it was a box-office smash in Poland. New publications, free of government censorship, appeared by the hundreds. One of the most influential of these was the union's weekly newsletter, *Solidarność*, edited by Tadeusz Mazowiecki, a Catholic lawyer and journalist who was to play an important part in Poland's later political history—and Walesa's.

Walesa was constantly on the go during this time. He went to Warsaw to meet with Cardinal Wyszynski. He spoke to hundreds of associations of factory workers and farmers in various parts of the country, and he proudly displayed in his office the souvenirs they gave him: a miner's headlamp, a statue of a steelworker, dolls wearing peasant clothing.

Nor was Walesa's activity confined to Poland. As an international celebrity, he was invited to visit other countries. He and Danuta, along with some of his advisers, went to France, Sweden, and Switzerland. They visited Italy, and Walesa had a private half-hour audience with the Pope.

Walesa was given a hero's welcome in all the countries he visited, but the country that most fascinated him was Japan. He found that the Japanese trade unionists were well organized, precise, and efficient; but he also felt that they were somewhat rigid, and he wondered whether Japanese culture placed sufficient value on individualism. In an effort to lighten up one formal meeting, he seized a pair of scissors and cut an official's tie in two. The Japanese found this prankishness somewhat obscure, but they were good sports about it.

One emotional high point during the first few months of Solidarity's existence was the dedication of a monument to the victims of the 1970 shipyard strike.

85

For a decade, Walesa had kept alive his dream of building this memorial. After the strike ended, workers set about designing and building it. It was constructed in the workshops of the Lenin Shipyard and erected just outside Gate Number 2. The monument is composed of three towering metal crosses that represent the strikes of 1956, 1970, and 1976, each bearing a black anchor, the wartime national symbol of Poland. It was dedicated on December 16, 1980, ten years after the 1970 shootings. The names of the fallen workers were read out, and after each name, the 150,000 people who had gathered for the ceremony cried out, "He is still with us." Representatives from the church, the party, and the union spoke about the need for Poles to bury the conflicts of the past and work together to build a secure future.

All the while, however, conflicts were building, both within Solidarity and between the union and the government. Many organizers and activists thought Walesa was moving too slowly. They also feared that he was losing the spirit of democracy when he started wearing a suit and tie to union meetings while everyone else wore plain shirts or sweaters. And he sometimes yawned openly or even fell asleep while people were talking.

The divisions among Solidarity's leadership went deeper, however, and were hard to bridge. Although Polish workers remained loyal to Walesa, whom they regarded as a national hero like Pilsudski, many of the other oppositionists grew impatient with him when he appealed to workers to cooperate with the government's economic plans and not go on strike. Some of them became angry. An economist named Stefan Kurowski, who had helped prepare economic proposals for Solidarity, complained of Walesa. "He has an enormous tendency to give in, to agree with the government." And Andrzej Gwiazda, an original WZZ organizer who had passed out leaflets with Walesa in the 1970s, was so disenchanted with his old friend's leadership that he called him "a dictatorial, vain fool" and "a blockhead with a mustache." A more measured criticism came from Mieczyslaw Lach, the leader of one of the regional Solidarity chapters, who said, "Walesa makes too many decisions himself. We often need clear, quick decisions, but he had gone too far."

For his part, Walesa truly believed that decisive individual leadership was vital, a conviction that was shaped by the failure of the 1970 strike, when three workers were shot. He felt a strong personal connection to the common people of Poland who placed their faith in him. He also believed that compromise was necessary, and argued that the union had to give the government some support. The Soviets were already unhappy about the Gdansk Agreement and fearful that the spirit of rebellion, which they called "the Polish disease," might spread to other Soviet-dominated countries in Eastern Europe. Many Poles, including Walesa, believed that if the Soviets thought the Polish government had lost control of the country they would send their army in to restore it. For this reason Walesa hoped to avoid a forceful direct attack on the government.

Walesa liked to compare the Polish state to a brick wall. "You can't knock the wall down by banging your head against it," he would say. "All you will have is a sore head. You have to go slowly, one brick at a time, one step at a time." But the more radical oppositionists, such as Jacek Kuron and Andrzej Gwiazda, felt that Walesa was giving away too much of the ground the strikers had gained. They were upset when, in his speech at the dedication of the shipyard monument, he urged his listeners to "keep peace and order, respect all laws and authorities, and show prudence and reflection in all actions."

Considerable tension among the Solidarity leaders existed by September 1981. That was when the union was scheduled to hold its first official congress, or national meeting, and elect a chairman for its national committee. Walesa was fairly certain that he would be elected, but he also knew there would be challenges from other candidates who were displeased with his leadership and with the state of Polish affairs in general.

Although the union had been in existence for a year, conditions in Poland had not improved very much. In some ways they had gotten worse. Gierek had been forced out of office as party secretary in the aftermath of the Gdansk Agreement. His replacement was Stanislaw Kania, who governed the country together with General Wojciech Jaruzelski, the prime minister and minister of defense. The new government dragged its feet about making the workers' demands law and putting them into practice.

The biggest disappointment, however, was that the economy grew steadily worse. Food, household goods, and fuel were in ever-shorter supply. Queuing, or lining up to shop, had always been part of Polish daily life, but now it reached bizarre proportions. Lines began forming at five in the morning. Some stores honored "night lists," where shoppers could reserve a place in the qucuc by signing a paper the night before. Apartment buildings formed cooperative groups whose members took turns queuing for one another. Shoppers with a bit of spare change hired children or old people to stand in line for them. The tedium and discomfort of queuing often ended in anger and dismay when shoppers finally got into a store, only to discover that it had little or nothing to sell.

As always in Poland, the economic disarray was reflected in public events. Wildcat strikes—spontaneous strikes that were not authorized by the union leaders—broke out all over Poland. The workers were angry that the government was not consulting them about economic policies, as it had promised to do. The government was angry that the workers were striking and further damaging the economy. To keep communication open between the two groups, Walesa urged workers not to strike, but many of his Solidarity colleagues thought his position was too moderate. In addition, some Solidarity spokespeople openly accused him of destroying the union's democracy by acting in a way that did not reflect the wishes of the majority.

Meanwhile, order in Poland was breaking down. The security police started arresting activists. Workers who were organizing Rural Solidarity, a farmers' union, were beaten by the militia. There were reports of Soviet tanks positioned on the borders of Poland and rumors that the Soviet Union might invade.

By the time the first Solidarity congress began, emotions were running high. Delegates questioned Walesa about a deal he had made with the government a few weeks earlier. In return for Walesa's agreement that the party could veto the union's nominations for plant manager, the Polish parliament had finally passed a law that allowed self-governing unions to exist. But some Solidarity members were angry that Walesa had made this deal after consulting only his trusted advisers, not the full national committee of the union. They also complained that the government's new veto power watered down the workers' ability to govern themselves. The congress turned into a debate over Walesa's leadership style, which many felt was high-handed and dictatorial.

Listening to speech after speech attacking his leadership, Walesa became frustrated. He had acted as he had because he believed the union's very existence was threatened, and he was fed up with having to explain his every move. When he and the other two candidates for the chairmanship were scheduled to hold a debate, Walesa said he was tired of talking. He held up his fists and said jokingly, with a big laugh, "Does anyone want to settle this with boxing gloves?"

The joke was on Walesa. He was elected to the post of union chairman, but by a narrow majority of only 55 percent of the votes. A year earlier he had had almost total support. It signaled to Walesa that his popularity had slipped badly, and that he was no longer in full control of Solidarity.

The question about Walesa's leadership was not the only problem that faced Solidarity by the end of 1981. The high hopes of August 1980 had gradually diminished as economic troubles hardened. In the midst of a particularly harsh winter, people grumbled more than ever about queuing and the lack of fuel. The twenty-one demands of the Gdansk Agreement had brought an exciting surge of *odnowa* to newspapers, theaters, and schools, but accomplished little in the mines and factories. After months of stalemate, tension between workers and the government had increased to a dangerous point. Walesa felt that the government and the union were about to collide head-on.

On November 4, Walesa and Cardinal Jozef Glemp, the head of the Polish Catholic church after the death of Cardinal Wyszynski, met with Jaruzelski in the hope of negotiating a compromise that would improve life in the troubled nation. They talked for two hours and twenty minutes, and for a time it seemed as though Jaruzelski might be willing to discuss social issues with Solidarity. The union members were restless and impatient. Most did not believe that the government meant to yield any control, no matter what anyone said. Not only had the government refused to share political power with the union, but government leaders were beginning to hint that the right to strike—the heart of the Gdansk Agreement—might be withdrawn.

Solidarity spokespeople grew increasingly radical, demanding political concessions, such as free parliamentary elections that would include candidates who were not Communist party members. Matters came to a head on the night of December 12. Radical members of the Solidarity National Commission debated whether or not to call a nationwide strike on the anniversary of the 1970 riots. Messages kept coming to union headquarters reporting the arrests of activists and ominous movements of the army and security police.

Suddenly the debate took a turn that gave the government the excuse it had been looking for to shut down the union. The more radical leaders of Solidarity called for a nationwide vote on whether the authorities were "fit to govern" the country. If the vote was negative, they proposed that Solidarity form a new government. In addition, the committee declared, Poland's military alliance with the Soviet Union should be renegotiated.

At this, Walesa threw both hands in the air in disgust. "Now you've done it," he cried angrily to his radical colleagues. What they were discussing went far beyond economic reform and union recognition. The government could easily interpret the debate as treason, which would be met with stern repression. Walesa knew that the end had come.

Around midnight the teletype machine in the union office fell silent. People looked at one another nervously and then picked up telephone receivers. The lines were dead. Everyone understood then that the government had shut down all communication between Gdansk and the outside world.

When Walesa left the meeting, he was deeply discouraged. He was convinced that after only 500 days, Solidarity was finished. He went home expecting to be arrested. "On the way home the snow began to fall heavily," he remembers. "Everything was silent."

8

Banned

WALESA'S DOORBELL BEGAN ringing as soon as he got home that night. The first people to arrive were from the RMP, the Young Poland Movement, who told Walesa that some of their colleagues had been arrested. Walesa counseled them to wait until morning and not take any rash actions that might bring about their own arrests. Next, the wife of Walesa's driver showed up in tears. Her husband had been arrested. While Danuta comforted her, Walesa reflected that his own arrest would probably be next.

A few moments later, the doorbell rang again. It was Tadeusz Fiszbach, the party secretary for Gdansk, and Jerzy Kolodziejski, the district governor. Although these two men were part of the state machine, Walesa had always gotten along fairly well with them. Now they seemed dazed by the events of the night, and they awkwardly told Walesa that he was wanted in Warsaw. He refused to leave his apartment until the Solidarity members who had been arrested were freed. Fiszbach

94

and Kolodziejski went off to confer with party headquarters in Warsaw by telephone.

Soon the doorbell jangled again. Peering through the peephole, Danuta could see a group of police carrying crowbars. They demanded to be let in and told her they had come for her husband. She refused to open the door, insisting that they must wait until Fiszbach and Kolodziejski returned. They agreed to wait. An hour later, the Gdansk party secretary and the district governor were back. Danuta opened the door and let the whole crowd of officials and police into the apartment. Walesa was in the bedroom, packing a suitcase. He knew what was coming.

Kolodziejski told Walesa that Jaruzelski had demanded his presence in Warsaw. "You'll be better off going on your own than being dragged there by force," the governor advised. Escorted by the local officials and a detachment of police, Walesa left the apartment at five-thirty. By nine in the morning, he was in Warsaw.

That morning, December 13, 1981, the people of Poland woke to find their country under martial law, which meant that the country was under military rule. At midnight, Wojciech Jaruzelski, who was now party secretary as well as prime minister, had called out the army and ordered tank columns into Warsaw, Gdansk, and other cities. Roads were blocked, telephone lines were cut, and armed guards patrolled the streets. Security officers arrested 600 Solidarity leaders and members.

At six in the morning, a message to the nation from

General Jaruzelski was broadcast on television and radio. He announced that he had imposed martial law in order to quell the "adventurists" (he meant Solidarity) who were threatening to destroy law and order and the unity of the state. He also proclaimed that martial law would remain in force until order and economic stability were restored. He and parliament then proceeded to pass a number of decrees that gave the government and the army full control over the people. Mail could be censored, phone conversations could be tapped, and all published and printed materials had to be approved by the government. No one was allowed to use printing equipment, even office copying machines, without permission from the party. No one was permitted on the streets between ten at night and six in the morning. Public meetings—except church services—were outlawed. The schools and universities were closed, and when they were reopened, they would be run by government-appointed administrators. All citizens were required to obey orders from the party or the military at all times. Anyone who resisted or who was thought to pose a threat to state security could be arrested and held for as long as the state wished. And finally, Solidarity's right to exist was suspended. Five hundred days of freedom had come to an end.

Many people think that Jaruzelski resorted to the harsh measure of imposing martial law in order to save Poland from a worse fate—military intervention by the Soviet Union. Jaruzelski has hinted at this, and such an outcome could well have happened. The Soviets had invaded Hungary in 1956 and Czechoslovakia in 1968 when those countries' communist regimes were threatened by public unrest.

Whatever the reason, Poles were filled with feelings of doom and despair. Their hopes for a more democratic government, for economic reforms, and above all for civil rights, such as free speech and a free press, had been swiftly crushed. It was a shocking blow after the heady excitement of 1980 and 1981. Many Poles who were out of the country when this "state of war" began simply defected—that is, they refused to return. Among these were Poland's ambassadors to the United States and Japan.

The world reacted in various ways to Jaruzelski's actions. The Soviet Union, not surprisingly, was pleased that he had acted to keep the communist government from toppling. But the United States and other democracies condemned Jaruzelski's maneuvers. Many nations placed economic sanctions on Poland, refusing to buy Polish goods or sell their own products to Poland. This, of course, made economic conditions in Poland worse. Eventually Walesa and other opposition leaders pleaded with the United States to lift the sanctions, feeling that they were doing more harm than good. Over the weeks and months following December 13, world leaders called for an end to martial law in Poland, but Jaruzelski was less concerned with world opinion than with proving to the Soviets that he had his country under strict control.

The Poles did not take martial law lying down. The declaration was met with strikes and riots in some cities. On December 16, the anniversary of the 1970

Riot police used fire hoses to attack demonstrators in Warsaw in May 1982, six months after martial law was declared. The demonstrators were carrying Solidarity posters and shouted, "Down with the junta." Although Solidarity was outlawed, activists kept the movement alive underground. MATS LUNDEGÅRD/PHOTOREPORTERS

Gdansk riots, battles between protesters and army troops raged in Gdansk and other cities. Within a week the army had crushed these protests.

Although Solidarity was banned, activists kept the movement alive underground. Bogdan Lis and other dissidents who had avoided arrest by disappearing, formed the Temporary Coordinating Commission (TKK in Polish) to organize strikes, boycotts, and demonstrations. At least 500 illegal newsletters were secretly printed and distributed. Every time the government shut down a printing press or copying machine, another came into existence somewhere else. And although the schools and universities were closely watched by the party to ensure that nobody read forbidden books or talked about forbidden subjects, the oppositionists found a way. Certain professors and students created the Flying University (TKN in Polish), a series of underground classes in banned subjects such as political history, reminiscent of defiance during the Nazi occupation. These classes were held in people's apartments and homes, and constantly moved from place to place to stay ahead of the police.

Poles found ways of expressing themselves too. The actors' union, for example, refused to perform for the state-owned television station, although this meant that the actors lost their jobs. All over Poland, Solidarity logos were furtively painted on walls by night, scrubbed off by the police the following day, and repainted at night. Party officials were serenaded with chants of "We want Lech, not Wojciech!"

Altogether, about 10,000 Poles were arrested during the "state of war." Many of them were held in jails or internment camps for a year or more. Walesa was taken to a villa outside Warsaw. He was treated well, and Danuta was allowed to visit him. Jaruzelski and other government leaders repeatedly offered him his freedom if he agreed to make a televised appeal to the public to remain calm and cooperate with the government. Walesa refused to do this. He succeeded in smuggling messages to his supporters out of the villa, so the government decided to isolate him further.

Walesa was moved to a house in the Arlamow region, where party officials and members of the *nomenklatura* had their luxurious vacation homes. The government took him there because it wanted people to believe that he was getting special treatment. In truth, his situation and treatment were better than those of most prisoners, but he had no choice in the matter.

At Arlamow, Walesa was given a small room. It was not a prison cell, but he was closely guarded at all times. He was not deprived of food or tortured. For the most part, in fact, he was ignored by the government. Someone managed to smuggle to him a copy of *Time* magazine for January 4, 1982, in which a long article declared Walesa "Man of the Year" for 1981. Danuta was permitted to continue her visits. His guards treated him decently. One of them was a security police official who lived in Gdansk with the Krols, in the same house where Walesa had boarded years earlier. Walesa always told this guard to say hello from him to his old landlord, and the guard did so.

100

The Walesas' seventh child, a daughter, was born in March 1982. Walesa asked for permission to attend her baptism, but did not receive it. However, 50,000 people crowded the streets around the church when Maria-Wiktoria Walesa was baptized. It was the largest public gathering during the declaration of martial law, and it was also a powerful gesture of encouragement for Walesa.

During Lech's internment at Arlamow, Danuta Walesa found her own life changing. A year and a half earlier, during the shipyard strike, she had seen her husband in a new role as a public hero. At that time, she felt he was growing away from her. "I realized life was going to be different from then on," she said later of her feelings. "Unknown territory stretched ahead of us both. Would it be for better or for worse?"

With Lech interned, possibly for a long time, Danuta discovered new strength within herself. She had seven children to take care of: the boys Bogdan, Slawek, Prze-mek, and Jarek, and the girls Magdalena, Anna, and Maria-Wiktoria (the couple's eighth child, a daughter named Brygida, was born later in the 1980s). Danuta did her best to fill Walesa's shoes during his internment because of her determination to support everything that her husband and the other Solidarity members had fought for. She did not want all their work and suffering to be in vain. She made speeches on his behalf and gave interviews to both the Western newspapers and the Polish underground newsletters. Although she was harassed by the authorities on a number of occasions, she was never arrested—probably because the government feared the enormous public outcry that would certainly be raised.

Walesa is proud of the way Danuta tried to keep his spirits up and the opposition movement alive while he was at Arlamow. He also admits that she was able to be a full-time parent and activist, a combination he never succeeded in achieving. Walesa is deeply devoted to his children. He recalls that during the 1970s his happiest moments were when he took the family for walks along the Gdansk beach near their apartment building, or into town to visit Danuta's aunt. But during the August 1980 strike, and then during the 500 days of Solidarity, he had had little time to spend with his family, so that Danuta had to shoulder the extra load. "Danuta is more of a hero than I am," he has said more than once.

Walesa had no idea how long he would be interned. The months dragged on. In October 1982, Poland's parliament voted to outlaw Solidarity, which had been "under suspension" since December 1981. Now the union, and all other independent unions, were illegal and forbidden to exist. The gains made in 1980 had been officially erased.

A few weeks later, in November, the government arrested most of the TKK leaders. Walesa then wrote Jaruzelski a letter offering to meet with him to discuss a solution to the problems in Poland. Some people have criticized him for writing the letter, accusing him of caving in to government pressure. Others, however, agreed with Walesa that after almost a year of martial law it was time for the oppositionists to try once more

102

to work with the government. Jaruzelski never replied to the letter, but in a sudden and surprising gesture, he released Walesa from Arlamow. Walesa's internment ended on November 12, 1982, after 11 months.

The government had effectively quelled numerous strikes and demonstrations during 1982, and many of the TKK leaders were still in prison, so perhaps Jaruzelski felt that the opposition movement had been sufficiently quashed and Walesa would be harmless. The main reason for Walesa's release, however, was that Jaruzelski wanted help from the West to bolster the economy. He needed to improve his standing in the eyes of Western leaders, and the best way to do that was to free the man who had become an international symbol of freedom.

Walesa returned to Gdansk. Rumors of his release had been circulating for several days, and he was greeted by thousands of people who had been waiting in the street outside his apartment building. In the following months, his comings and goings were regularly noted by the security police. He was placed under house arrest on December 16 so that he could not take part in the ceremony at Lenin Shipyard to commemorate the 1970 strike. In April 1983 he was allowed to return to his old job. His reception at Lenin Shipyard reassured him that he had not lost his place in the hearts of his fellow workers. On his first day, thousands of them shook his hand or asked for his autograph. A few months later, when fans at a football game recognized Walesa sitting in the stands, 40,000 of them began shouting "Walesa!" and "Long live Soli-

darity!" The "disturbance" forced the government television station to cut short its coverage of the game.

Martial law was formally lifted in July 1983. It did
not change much. Jaruzelski's parliament had passed
laws that undid all the progress that Solidarity had
made. But the Solidarity movement and Walesa had
made an impression on the world that could not be
erased. In recognition of his contribution to freedom
and human rights, Walesa was awarded the International Peace Prize of the Nobel Prize Committee in October 1983. Although he was moved and honored by
this acknowledgment of his work for Solidarity, Walesa
decided not to go to Norway to accept the prize. He was
fairly certain that the authorities would let him leave
Poland, but he was not at all certain that they would let
him return. So Danuta went to Oslo on his behalf to
accept the medal.

Danuta Walesa's trip to Oslo made news headlines
around the world. Walesa admits that he was a bit
worried about how she would speak and act in front of
the cameras, and that he was also a little jealous when
he watched her on television and saw all the attention
she received. He and Father Jankowski listened to the
Nobel ceremony on a radio in Jankowski's parish
church. Bohdan Cywinski, a Solidarity activist and
newsletter editor, had accompanied Danuta, and he
delivered the formal speech of acceptance that Walesa
had written. Then Danuta spoke.

"I would like to express my gratitude to the illustri-
ous representatives of the people of Norway for provid-
ing proof that we still live, and proof that our ideals are

104

still strong, by awarding the Nobel Peace Prize to the president of Solidarity," she said.

Says Walesa, "My heart melted when I heard Danuta's voice coming to me from so far away. . . . It was one of the most beautiful moments of my life."

The Peace Prize was, as Danuta had said, proof that Solidarity was not dead. Throughout 1982 and 1983, opposition activity had continued, becoming more open when the authorities seemed to be looking the other way, and then disappearing underground again when they cracked down. Walesa stayed fairly clear of the TKK, although he approved of many of its activities. In April 1983 he arranged a secret three-day meeting with underground oppositionists. When Walesa and the TKK published an account of it in the underground newsletters, the government was embarrassed that the most visible oppositionist in Poland had eluded the secret police for three days. After that, Walesa and other known oppositionists were repeatedly pulled into police headquarters for questioning.

Walesa decided not to provoke the government so openly. In the eyes of the state, he was now an ordinary private citizen, not a union chairman, but he hoped that if he could stay out of serious trouble he might one day have a chance to get the union started again. He did, however, give interviews and make public appearances, during which he tried to appear firm, hopeful, patriotic, and cautious, all at the same time.

In 1984, the government stepped up its persecution of opposition activists. The crackdown culminated in October, when Father Jerzy Popieluszko, a priest who had openly criticized the government and supported Solidarity, was murdered by members of the security police. Popieluszko's funeral became a demonstration of public outrage. Solidarity banners waved in the breeze. Walesa said at the graveside, "Solidarity lives, because you gave your life for us." He said of that occasion later, "I felt the crowd swell with confidence. I felt their faith in moral values strengthened, their faith in the necessity of realizing these values in society. The more this conviction spread, the stronger would be our defense against evil, against the pitfalls of chaos and despair."

Yet Walesa also felt that tension was building. The economy remained in dire shape. The government seemed more hostile to the opposition than it had been before the 1980 strike. Soon after the funeral, Walesa was quoted in an underground newsletter as saying that the government was waging "a ruthless struggle against any reconciliation or agreement."

Walesa feared an outbreak of renewed violence on both sides, rebellion and repression that might result in a Soviet invasion. However, the first hint of change came within a year, and from a most unlikely direction—the Soviet Union.

9

A New Beginning

IN THE SPRING of 1985, a new leader came to power in the Soviet Union. His name was Mikhail Gorbachev, and in the late 1980s he introduced new policies in the Soviet Union. He called these *glasnost* (openness) and *perestroika* (restructuring the economy). This meant freer speech, a more participatory form of government, an economy that permitted some forms of private enterprise and private ownership, and a general loosening of the Soviet Communist party's hold on the people. In addition to changing things in the Soviet Union, that country began to loosen its grip on Eastern Europe, encouraging Eastern bloc nations to attempt economic reforms.

In 1986, Jaruzelski took two important steps. First, he began allowing the state-censored newspapers to print the truth about Poland's economic situation so that the people would have access to the facts. This was something that Solidarity had demanded back in 1980. Second, he released all political prisoners and declared that there would be no further political ar-

107

rests: "No one in our country is or will be discriminated against for his or her convictions," he announced.

The opposition was unsure how to respond to Jaruzelski's moves. Some Solidarity leaders, including Walesa, believed that the oppositionists might have a chance to work with the government to achieve reforms. The official leader of the Polish Catholic church, Jozef Cardinal Glemp, shared this view. But other oppositionists, including many younger people who had come of age during the "state of war," felt that Solidarity should remain underground and stick to its earlier position: no cooperation with the government until the Gdansk Agreement was fully enacted.

This difference of opinion reflected a division between the moderate and radical elements of Solidarity. While everyone agreed that the movement should continue to push for reform, not everyone agreed on methods. Walesa and his close advisers believed in a conservative, one-step-at-a-time approach, while others felt that it was important to continue holding strikes and demonstrations until all the demands of the Gdansk Agreement, including civil-rights reforms, were restored and enacted into law.

The oppositionists agreed, however, that it was time to bring Solidarity back into existence. Although the union was still officially outlawed, the growing openness in Poland encouraged Walesa to form a Solidarity Provisional Council in September 1987, with him as its chairman.

Economic conditions had worsened throughout 1987. In November, Jaruzelski asked the people of Po-

108

land to vote on whether or not they would accept a new economic reform program that would mean harder times for all in the immediate future, but might improve the economy in the long run. Walesa and his advisers decided that they could not support the government because it made no provision for the workers to take part in the planning process and because the details of the program were not very clear. The word went out that Walesa and Solidarity wanted people to boycott the vote—that is, not vote at all. About a third of Poland's eligible voters stayed away from the polls.

Nearly 70 percent of the people who were eligible to vote in Jaruzelski's referendum did so, however, and more than half of them voted in favor of the government's proposed plan. But the election laws defined a majority as 51 percent of all eligible voters, not just of those who actually vote, so neither side could really claim a victory. Because of the boycott, however, Jaruzelski failed to get a majority vote backing his reforms.

The planned 110-percent increase in food prices was reduced to a 40-percent increase, which took effect in early 1988. Because people's salaries had fallen by an average of about 20 percent since the beginning of the 1980s, many Poles now found themselves worse off than they had been before Solidarity. As had happened so often in the past, the price increases triggered a wave of strikes. Before long the country was experiencing the worst unrest since the declaration of martial law.

Workers went on strike at the huge steelmaking complex at Nowa Huta in southern Poland, at weapons plants near Krakow, and—once again—in the ship-yards of Gdansk. Walesa had not encouraged or au-thorized the strikes, but he did not discourage them either. In Gdansk, some 3,000 workers occupied the Lenin Shipyard, draped Gate Number 2 with Solidarity banners, and demanded higher wages and the legal-ization of Solidarity.

At times, the 1988 strike managed to re-create the excitement and optimism that had fueled the 1980 strike. One exhilarating moment occurred when An-drzej Gwiazda read the workers a telegram that had arrived at the Lenin Shipyard from their fellow strikers at the Lenin Steelworks in Nowa Huta: "One Lenin started this," it said, "and two Lenins will finish it." The crowd cheered wildly. Yet the overall mood of the strike was somber. Many of the younger oppositionists were more desperate than hopeful. They wanted radical re-form and their catchphrase was "Shoot or emigrate"—that is, be prepared for violent struggle or leave the country. Many of the older workers, on the other hand, were disillusioned. They hoped only for a decent wage increase and no longer shared Solidarity's earlier dreams of far-reaching reform. Most people were somewhere in the middle.

Walesa, too, appeared to be somewhere in the mid-dle. As the head of the still-banned union, he withheld formal approval of the strike, but he did take part in it and was even shut inside the yard when police bar-ricaded it in May. He was now 44 years old, and to many he seemed tired and rather ordinary, less pas-sionate than the Walesa they remembered. When he

Lech Walesa addressed striking shipyard workers at the Lenin Shipyard in Gdansk in 1988. With economic conditions in Poland getting worse and social order breaking down, in 1989 the communist government was forced to legalize Solidarity again. REUTERS/BETTMANN

addressed the workers he repeated his message of perseverance and moderation: "If we do not make reforms peacefully and with compromises, then we are threatened with a revolution and a bloody one," he warned.

The government struck back at the strikers with force. In Nowa Huta, riot police used clubs and percussion grenades to break up the strike. The Gdansk workers were afraid that the same thing could happen there. The strain grew so great that one worker tried to commit suicide. After nine days, Walesa told the strikers that they were not getting anywhere and should disband peacefully. They did so, but they struck again in August, when the government raised food prices once more and a new wave of unrest rocked the country. But this time was different. Jaruzelski and the government were finally willing to admit that they could not repair the economy or control the population without Solidarity's help. Jaruzelski invited Walesa and other members of the opposition to begin debates with the government.

To Walesa, this invitation was a victory. At last, after years of trying to win the right to participate in economic decision making, the way seemed open. He urged workers to end the strikes and give the talks a chance to work, but progress stalled when the government refused to legalize Solidarity again. There was also tension among Solidarity leaders, some of whom felt that Walesa had once more gone too far by accepting Jaruzelski's offer without consulting the others.

At the beginning of 1989, things were as bad as ever. But it proved to be a year of surprises for Poland—

112

indeed, for all of Eastern Europe. Largely because of Mikhail Gorbachev's hands-off policy, the Soviet Union eased its grip on its allies in Eastern Europe, and anticommunist movements broke out in those countries. Hungary tore down the barbed wire barrier along its border with Austria, and thousands of people from Eastern European countries fled through the newly opened border to the West. Hungary's government proceeded to cut its ties with the Soviet Union. The Berlin Wall, the best-known symbol of the Iron Curtain, which had divided communist Eastern Europe from the noncommunist West since 1961, was torn down by East German government construction crews, paving the way for the people of East and West Germany to meet freely—and for the two countries to reunite. Pro-democracy demonstrations in Czechoslovakia brought about the downfall of the communist government there. A popular uprising in Romania overthrew a brutal dictator. In every way, it was a year of sweeping changes and new beginnings for the people of Eastern Europe. But the first changes happened in Poland.

In April, under pressure from all sides to salvage the economy and break the deadlock of Polish politics, Jaruzelski legalized Solidarity and invited the union to join him in forming a coalition government, a government that would include both Solidarity and the Communist party. This step was both unexpected and welcome. It was the fulfillment of Walesa's long-held dream of change. It also marked Solidarity's emergence as a genuine political party.

113

To ensure that the communists would not lose power entirely, Jaruzelski had Poland's constitution changed. Instead of one chamber, the Sejm, parliament was to have two chambers, the 460-seat Sejm and a new 100-seat Senate; together they would be called the National Assembly. The Senate seats were open to all candidates, but 299 seats in the Sejm were reserved for the Communist candidates of the PZPR and candidates of several small parties that were PZPR allies. Another constitutional change added a presidency, so that Poland would have both a prime minister and a president, both to be elected by the National Assembly. The Communists were to get one post and Solidarity the other. But the constitution also declared that nationwide popular elections for a president would be held no later than 1995, and it was clear that the role of president was expected to become much more important at that time.

Elections for the National Assembly were held in June. Solidarity was swept to victory, winning all 161 of the available seats in the Sejm and 99 of the 100 Senate seats. It was a stunning victory for Solidarity and a humiliating defeat for the Communist party. "Our defeat is total," Jaruzelski told other party leaders. The National Assembly elected Jaruzelski president. Now the question was: Who would be the country's prime minister?

Many Poles expected that Walesa would automatically become their new prime minister. Solidarity had circulated a pamphlet calling for members of the small parties allied with the PZPR to join them in "a government of national responsibility headed by Lech Walesa." But Walesa held back for several reasons. He knew that if he became prime minister, the remaining Communist members of the Sejm and their supporters might turn against the new government, feeling that it had lost too much power to Solidarity's best-known leader. He also felt that it would be prudent to hold himself in reserve—that way, if the new government faltered or Solidarity's leadership seemed weak, Walesa would still have the support of the public and might be able to save the day by stepping in. Furthermore, he hinted that he was more interested in running for president in 1995 than in becoming prime minister right away, before the new government had a chance to prove itself.

Some observers have also suggested that Walesa simply did not like the idea of facing all the details, problems, and decisions of day-to-day administration, preferring to remain in a loosely defined position of power where he could do what he likes best—inspire the people of Poland and serve as their spokesman. Walesa agreed to work with Jaruzelski to find a candidate for prime minister who would represent Solidarity and still be acceptable to the non-Solidarity members of parliament.

Their choice was Tadeusz Mazowiecki, the Solidarity leader who had edited the weekly newsletter *Solidarność*. He had been one of Walesa's advisers during the founding of Solidarity and had spent a year in jail during martial law. On August 25, Mazowiecki stepped into his new job as Poland's prime minister. He was the

115

first noncommunist prime minister in Eastern Europe in 40 years.

Mazowiecki was not the only former oppositionist with a new post in government. Jacek Kuron was named minister of labor and Adam Michnik was elected to the Senate. Walesa held no official position in the government, but remained as president of the newly reorganized Solidarity. Most Poles felt that the changes of 1989 would never have come about without him. "It is an incredible success for our struggle," he said, referring to the fact that Poland had just formed the first noncommunist government in any Soviet-bloc country. Then Walesa added a typically cautionary note: "But now let us see it in practice."

116

10

President Walesa

A S WALESA HAD predicted, the Solidarity government had its work cut out for it. Conditions
in Poland were very bad. Its air, water, and soil
pollution were among the worst in the industrial
world. Environmental experts estimated that 11 percent of the country, occupied by 35 percent of the people, was in a state of ecological breakdown. Lung
disease and other pollution-related illnesses were
rampant, and the life expectancy of the average Pole
had decreased since the early 1970s, down to just
under 40 years—again, one of the lowest figures in the
industrial world. Crime was on the increase. Poland
also has a high rate of alcoholism, with about 1,500
deaths and 10,000 injuries each year from drunken
driving. Doctors and researchers believe that Poland's
rising rates of alcoholism, crime, and illness are
closely linked to the stress and depression that many
Poles experience because of economic and political
conditions. By 1989, the number of people who sought

medical help for psychological problems was increasing by about 30 percent each year.

The economy was the most serious problem that Mazowiecki and the new government had to face. Poland owed $40 billion to foreign countries. High inflation was lowering the buying power of the *zloty*, the Polish currency, every day. Prices were going up, incomes were stagnant or coming down, and unemployment was on the rise. Economic collapse seemed imminent.

The government took some immediate and drastic steps. The state-run economy that Poland had had since World War II was replaced by a free-market system like that of the United States and other Western nations, in which manufacturers and farmers can decide for themselves what they will produce, whom they will sell to, and how much to charge for it. To ease the period of transition from one type of economy to the other, Poland's new leaders passed laws that linked wages to the cost of living. In other words, workers were to receive pay increases that would keep up with increases in the cost of food and other basic goods. But when the government controls on food pricing were eliminated, prices shot up by 78 percent in a single month, and the government simply did not have the funds to provide corresponding pay hikes. Government subsidies—payments that had kept the cost of housing artificially low, or allowed many farmers to stay in business by paying high prices for their produce—were eliminated, bringing great hardship. The cost of living soared, and the standard of living dropped.

Mazowiecki and the other members of government found themselves saying just what Jaruzelski, Gierek, and other Communist party leaders had said before them: economic reform takes time; things cannot get better overnight; be patient and give our program a chance to work. Meanwhile, many discontented Poles wondered when they would start to reap the benefits of their big reforms.

And what about Lech Walesa, the man who, in the eyes of many, had brought about the downfall of communism in Poland? Although he hinted many times that he had played his part and had no interest in politics now that Solidarity had been reborn, no one really believed these protests. Most Solidarity leaders, and other people who knew Walesa, felt that he still considered himself Poland's real leader. Many Polish men and women, remembering the 1980 strike, agreed.

In April 1990, Walesa was re-elected to the post of union president at Solidarity's first official national congress since 1981. That election came as no surprise. But many Solidarity members were surprised when, that same month, Walesa began saying that the government should schedule a presidential election sooner than 1995. Less than a year after Mazowiecki had taken office as prime minister, Walesa appeared to be criticizing his former ally.

All at once, Walesa, who had often counseled his

119

hot-headed oppositionist colleagues to be patient and work with the existing system, was saying, "It is necessary to speed up the pace of reform and demolish the old structures." A number of Poles began to wonder whether Walesa was motivated by genuine concern, or by a desire for power. Some speculated that he had grown tired of being a shadowy background figure while Mazowiecki held the official leadership post.

Adam Bromke, a university professor and former oppositionist who is a member of the Polish Academy of Sciences, said about Walesa, "He is having to share a stage that was once his alone, and he doesn't like it." Walesa was also accused of being an opportunist, of taking advantage of the economic problems that plagued Mazowiecki's government to advance his own ambitions.

Whatever his reasons for urging an immediate election, Walesa's position caused consternation among his Solidarity colleagues, as he must have known it would. One minister in Mazowiecki's cabinet said bluntly, "He seems prepared to put everything we have achieved this year at risk to further his personal ambitions." Mazowiecki declared that moving the presidential elections ahead of schedule would disorganize the government and upset the economic reform program that had just been put into place.

The growing tension between the two former allies, Walesa and Mazowiecki, became a public rift when Walesa began openly criticizing Mazowiecki for moving too slowly with economic reform and for being too soft on communists who still held government posts.

Those who accused Walesa of opportunism pointed out that these are exactly the sentiments that would most appeal to the masses of Poland's working people, who were eager to see progress. And Walesa did not seem to have concrete suggestions of his own to offer.

Events accelerated when Poland's Communist president, General Jaruzelski, announced his resignation in September—even though he could have remained in his post until 1995. The National Assembly voted to schedule a presidential election for November 25, 1990, and candidates began to declare themselves. The top contenders were Walesa and Mazowiecki. All at once the campaign was on—the first campaign in Poland's history for a president to be elected by the vote of the people.

Like candidates from rival political parties in the United States and other democracies, Walesa and Mazowiecki began crisscrossing the country, making speeches to woo voters. Walesa, who had a natural ability to speak to the hearts of his listeners, was a more successful speaker. He addressed crowds and rallies with his trademark blend of humor, patriotic appeals, personal anecdotes, and folk wisdom. He criticized the Mazowiecki government and painted bright pictures of a glorious future. Crowds loved his rhetoric, but some analysts wondered just what his plans for governing the country really were. When asked what he would do if he was elected, Walesa tended to respond in vague terms. "There will be a lot of improvisation," he told one reporter. "I'll travel around and check things."

121

Mazowiecki, on the other hand, urged that economic reforms proceed at a measured, thoughtful pace. He pointed out that the U.S. government and the World Bank had agreed to help Poland with aid, which was a vote of confidence in his government's ability to turn the economy around. He warned audiences that persecution of former communist leaders would be a violation of Solidarity's commitment to human rights—"a witch-hunt," he called it. And, in an ugly reminder that anti-Semitism has not disappeared from Poland, Mazowiecki, a lifelong Catholic, was forced to confront persistent rumors that he is of Jewish descent.

Indeed, anti-Semitism played a disturbing part in the presidential campaign. The Polish people's fervent Catholicism has sometimes included anti-Semitic elements, and the communists promoted anti-Semitism as well for their own purposes, especially in the 1960s. At times it seemed that Walesa was making an appeal to the intolerant aspects of the national character—when, for example, he boasted at a rally that he was "a true Pole, with documents to prove it." In his speeches, he repeatedly called upon "Jews in the government" to identify themselves. Some of his supporters took to scrawling the Star of David—the international symbol of Judaism—on Mazowiecki's campaign posters. The Western press responded with sharp criticism, and Walesa quickly apologized for his remarks, saying that they had been misunderstood. Still, many people found it a disappointing aspect of Poland's new democratic process.

Walesa's campaign style placed him firmly in the

Polish tradition of strong, authoritarian leaders like Marshal Pilsudski, leaders who governed by personal appeal and did not feel obliged to seek legislative or popular support for everything they wanted to do. Some of Walesa's ideas seemed positively undemocratic, or at least unclear. He remarked at one point that Poland should have compulsory voting—that is, that everyone should be forced by law to vote. Later he said that this remark, like his talk of "Jews in government," had been misunderstood.

For much of his life, Walesa has been one of the world's boldest advocates of democracy and fair play. During the campaign, however, some observers felt he had one foot in the old conservative past and the other in the new democratic order.

The campaign aroused strong feelings and divided the Solidarity leadership into pro-Walesa and anti-Walesa factions. Walesa seemed to view it as a contest between the worker and the intellectual, a split that echoed the days before Solidarity united the oppositionist movement. Some of Walesa's former friends and supporters turned against him, saying he was too autocratic—too fond of taking matters into his own hands—to be a democratic president. Some even warned that he might become a dictator, who would insist upon total control of the government.

Adam Michnik, the KOR organizer who worked with Walesa in the early days of Solidarity, called Walesa "malicious, antagonistic, and dangerous" and compared him to Juan Perón, the popular Argentinian president whose autocratic rule became a dic-

123

tatorship. Others did not doubt Walesa's democratic convictions, but wondered whether this fiery, rabble-rousing union organizer possessed the patience and diplomacy required of a president. One newspaper asked about Walesa, "He can lead—but can he govern?"

The biggest surprise in the election campaign came from Canada. Stanislaw Tyminski was a Pole who left Poland in 1969 and went to Canada, where he studied computers and founded his own $5-million-a-year software company. He also had business interests in Peru. He returned to Poland and declared himself a presidential candidate, promising voters a "democracy of money."

Walesa's and Mazowiecki's supporters were quick to point out that Tyminski had contributed nothing to the struggle for freedom in Poland. While Solidarity members were striking and being jailed, Tyminski was living the good life in the West, and therefore he had not earned a leadership role. Yet Tyminski had undeniable popularity. After years of hard times and bleak prospects, audiences loved his success story, and they cheered at his assurances that he could bring capitalism and money-making opportunities to Poland. In a very short time, this candidate who had appeared out of nowhere—"a man from Mars," as Walesa indignantly called him—had climbed to third place in the pre-election polls, after Walesa and Mazowiecki.

One issue that none of the candidates wanted to discuss during the election was abortion. During the decades of communist rule, abortion was legal and

Solidarity leader Lech Walesa, accompanied by his wife Danuta (l) and his son Slawek (r) cast their votes in Poland's first democratic presidential election since the beginning of World War II. REUTERS/BETTMANN

readily available. Because contraceptives were not available in Poland, it was the primary method of birth control. And even though most Poles belong to the Roman Catholic church, which opposes any form of birth control, surveys have shown that the majority of Poles believed that women should have the right to make their own reproductive decisions.

Walesa is personally opposed to birth control and abortion, and he is also a very conservative Catholic who would like to increase the church's role in politics. This led many to wonder if he would support a move by the Catholic church to outlaw abortion. He tried to avoid answering that question because he did not want to upset voters who believed in abortion rights, but he finally had to admit that as a good Catholic he could not oppose the church's teachings. Mazowiecki, when pressed, said the same thing. It appeared to many observers that the church was going to experience a surge of political power in Poland no matter who won the election. This made people wonder whether efforts would be made to legislate other traditional Catholic values into law. Because separation between church and state is an important principle of democracy, the growth of the Catholic church's political power seemed to be a contradiction of the new democracy the Polish people had fought so hard for.

When election day came on November 25, 1990, everyone was surprised. According to election rules, a majority of 51 percent of all eligible voters was necessary to win. If no candidate won a majority, the top two candidates would have to hold a run-off election.

Walesa won the largest share of the vote, 39 percent, but failed to get the majority that had been forecast by opinion polls. What surprised everyone was that Mazowiecki, who had been expected to come in second, came in third with 20 percent. The second-place winner was the dark horse, Tyminski, with 23 percent. Walesa would now have to face Tyminski in a run-off election on December 9.

Mazowiecki accepted the verdict of the voters and announced that he was ready to retire from politics. "Society has made a choice," he said, not without bitterness. Walesa, too, displayed some bitterness. He complained about the indignity of having to compete with a "nobody," and he told an American reporter, "It's incomprehensible that after 20 years abroad this deserter could become the First Citizen."

In the end, when the Poles went to the polls in December to choose their new president, they did not pick the flashy newcomer. They voted for one of their own. They elected Walesa, whom many of them credited with making the elections possible in the first place. Despite questions about his philosophy of leadership and his qualifications to serve as president, to many Poles, Lech Walesa *is* freedom. In voting for him, they were voting for the new hope that he and Solidarity had brought to their troubled land.

Walesa promised not to let them down. "This is a victory not for me but for all of Poland," he declared joyously. "I will serve you all."

The new president-elect realized that he faced difficult challenges. Among the issues he had to deal with were the questions of abortion and women's rights in a free society, the eradication of anti-Semitism, the role of the church in Polish life and the separation of church and state, and above all the economic crisis that was devouring the country. The Polish people had learned to measure a government's effectiveness by economic measures, and they had also learned that they possessed the power to overturn governments.

On the political front, Walesa was confronted with the fact that not everyone supported him in his new presidential role. He had trouble choosing a prime minister. His first two choices, Mazowiecki and a Solidarity lawyer named Jan Olszewski, turned him down. Finally, a radical economist named Kristof Bieclecki accepted the post. But the splits that had occurred between various factions of Solidarity were indications that Poland was on its way to developing multiple political parties, and Walesa will almost certainly not be able to count on the backing of a single, unified Solidarity. For the time being, however, it was enough to know that he had been the people's final choice for president.

Saturday, December 22, 1990, was a historic day in Poland. Before a packed crowd in the parliament building in Warsaw, a 47-year-old electrician was sworn in as the nation's first freely elected president. On hand was 70-year-old Ryszard Kaczorowski, a representative of the surviving members of the Polish government-in-exile, the free Polish government that had existed before the 1939 Nazi invasion.

For 50 years, that government had remained in London, supported by about 150,000 Poles who lived in Great Britain. Its successive presidents-in-exile had proudly cherished some relics from the Pilsudski era of the 1920s and 1930s: the red presidential banner, the official seals of the president and the state, the president's ceremonial sashes, and the original text of the constitution of 1935. Kaczorowski carried these relics to Warsaw for the inauguration of Poland's first noncommunist president since the Nazi invasion.

"Walesa was chosen in a free election," Kaczorowski said, "so I decided to give him the symbols that we had been holding since the war."

Walesa blinked back tears as he was handed these symbols of the Polish state. Then, with Danuta and their children looking on, along with all the members of the National Assembly, Lech Walesa took the oath of office. The man who had once dreaded the prospect of life as a peasant farmer had become the president of his nation.

Earlier, Walesa had written, "I sometimes feel as if I belong to a past age, the age which is evoked in our national anthem, 'Poland Has Not Perished.' " Now, like the heroes of that bygone age, Lech Walesa can truly be said to have shaped Poland's history. He has served Poland as a soldier, a worker, a unionist, a political prisoner, an underground activist, and the elder statesman of the labor movement. Now he has taken on a new role. The man who once helped lead the fight against the government is now leading the government.

Lech Walesa must grapple with and solve serious

129

economic, social, and environmental problems, threats that are as grave as any that confronted the Polish heroes of bygone eras. It remains to be seen how he will face those threats and what kind of Poland he will help to create.

In becoming president of Poland, Walesa has embarked on an adventure that in many ways is bolder and more dangerous than the one he started in 1980 when he jumped atop a bulldozer to make a speech at the Lenin Shipyard. The stakes are higher, the consequences greater. And just as the workers' strike in 1980 riveted international attention on Poland, the world's eyes are focused on that country, and President Lech Walesa, once again.

Other books you might enjoy reading

1. Berry, Lynn. *Wojciech Jaruzelski.* New York: Chelsea House, 1990.

2. Craig, Mary. *The Crystal Spirit: Lech Walesa and His Poland.* London: Hodder and Stoughton, 1986.

3. Eringer, Robert. *Strike for Freedom: The Story of Lech Walesa and Polish Solidarity.* New York: Dodd, Mead, 1982.

4. Garton Ash, Timothy. *The Polish Revolution: Solidarity.* New York: Vintage Books, 1985.

5. Kaye, Tony. *Lech Walesa.* New York: Chelsea House, 1989.

6. Michnik, Adam. *Letters from Prison and Other Essays.* Berkeley: University of California Press, 1987.

7. Walesa, Lech. *A Way of Hope.* New York: Henry Holt, 1987.

8. Weschler, Lawrence. *The Passion of Poland: From Solidarity through the State of War.* New York: Pantheon Books, 1984.

ABOUT THE AUTHOR

Rebecca Stefoff has written more than fifty nonfiction books for young adults, including twenty biographies, many of contemporary world leaders. She lives in Philadelphia.

Printed in the United States
by Baker & Taylor Publisher Services